The Temple o
A Road to Spirit

One Woman's Journey
From Personal and Professional Despair
                    To Spiritual Awakening

A Memoir
A Near Death Experience Chronicled

Lee Papa

Las Vegas, NV
Web: www.leepapa.com
www.ganeshacenter.com
Email: lee@leepapa.com
lee@ganeshacenter.com

Dearest Cherry,
May you always Know
The Slipstream!
With Love,
Lee

The Temple of All Knowing, A Road to Spirit
By Lee Papa

Published by:
Light Source Publishing
Phone: 702-485-4985 | Website: www.leepapa.com
Copyright © 2014 Lee Papa | First Edition: March, 2014

The intent of this material is to provide general information to help your quest for emotional and spiritual growth. The author and publisher of this book do not dispense medical advice or prescribe any technique as a form of treatment for physical or emotional problems and therefore assume no responsibility for your actions.

Illustrations & Cover At by Shane Dieter of transpyre.com

Photography by Images by Edi of imagesbyedi.com

Design by Didier Ciambra of ciambraphotography.com

Printed in the United States of America
ISBN 978-1-62217-125-5

DEDICATIONS

For Paul Isensee –
Without your dedication, friendship, unwavering faith, and amazing culinary delights, my world would be far less flavorful.

For my son –
Your love and light shines the way for me each and every day. Thank you for being my beacon.

DISCLAIMER

The primary purpose of this manuscript is to open the window a crack or the door of your spiritual house to the possibilities that lie beyond your potential limiting beliefs regarding health and wellbeing – Mind – Body and Spirit.

The information provided in this manuscript is not intended to diagnose, cure, prevent or treat illness or disease of any kind.

This material is not for the purpose of replacing any medical treatment. Use what resonates, leave the rest. The core intended purpose of this material is to inspire based on experiences by the author.

Lee Papa, or anyone associated with Lee's manuscript or wellness center, Ganesha Center make no claims whatsoever and assume no liability of any kind for the misinterpretation or mis-use of this information, either written or implied.

ACKNOWLEDGEMENTS

The best way to find yourself is to lose yourself in the service of others

~Mahatma Gandhi~

This book felt like it was predestined or preordained by a realm that I could not see. However, it was 4 years in the making. On many occasions, I would be asked, "how is the book coming along," by my spiritual advisors, Great Grandmother and Sharon Bridwell. Their encouragement kept pushing me forward and their guidance and love are beyond compare.

There are many whom I would like to thank that have been associated in large and subtle ways with this story, and the subsequent manuscript. Although not everyone will be mentioned, I hold immense gratitude in my heart for all of them.

Firstly, my deepest gratitude to Source, Creator, the Universe, God, the Divine for all the love and guidance I received from the non-physical realm. Becoming awakened to my true nature, that of a spiritual being, is the greatest gift I could have received.

To my mother, for being the most amazing player in my life, who offered me the greatest opportunity for growth and expansion. I look forward to our continued communication. I love you mom!

Paul Isensee, with love and appreciation for all that you are. Thank you for being my right and left arms, for making everything so beautiful. Don't want to take this train without you! Here's to stopping to smell the flowers - parrot tulips.

My deep appreciation goes to Didier, for his extraordinary gifts. Not only is he the incredible father to our son, but I will always call him my dear friend and my guidance counselor. Didier shows his spiritual light through his spectacular photography and he can lay out a book like no other. Thank you for everything you do and everything you are. I love you.

Margaret "Mars" Roberts, of Rio Sierra Riverhouse, in Three Rivers, CA, thank you for skillfully guiding me through the initial edits – cut – cut – cut. Your authenticity, friendship and generosity will show me the way to my happy place at the inn, always.

Brenda Calvin your friendship, guidance, love, and encouragement to be true to myself, and seek balance will forever be in my heart, along with our extraordinary experiences together. With a song in my heart and laughter on my lips, I love you friend. Thank you for being my wing-woman!

To Wendy Fleming, thank you for the coaching, the love, the friendship and the laughter in the early days of the birth of my awakening. You believed in me and supported me, when there was a ghost town of encouragement.

To all the many, many volunteers who have supported, Reiki by Lee and Ganesha Center. You shall be blessed 100 fold for your service to mankind. My cup runneth over with appreciation.

Maria Abeloff, your encouragement, unconditional love and support have helped me through many a challenging time. You always have faith in me – thank you for seeing me – knowing me. Love, Hot-dog.

With appreciation in my heart, I acknowledge my friend Jane Tani. For your friendship has been a beautiful gift in my life. Your love, support and laughter during my journey has brightened the special chapters of my life.

To dear Tiffany Parks for your positivity, skill, precision, keeping us always on track, you are an alchemist in the most beautiful way.

Sari Grossman, for your love and support and for helping me review the early stages of the book.

Joan Peck, for always loving and believing in me. You are an inspiration! Your skill and patience editing the final manuscript helped me shine the message of what my heart wanted to share.

Joyce Mochrie, my appreciation goes to you for the careful editing and proofreading. I so appreciate you professionalism, kindness, and efficiency.

To Shane Dieter, thank you for being my mirror. When I had no words to express what I wanted to show on the book cover, you tapped-in to create, from the Oneness of Source. The design gave me chills and brought tears to my eyes. That confirmed it was exactly what I would have designed, if I had the creative gift myself.

To the thousands of individuals I have had the privilege of encountering, assisting, and working with in the capacity of being the Founder of Ganesha Center, I am most grateful for your allowing me into your healing and spiritual expansion process. I have loved every minute of being in service in this manner, and I am looking forward to the next phases of this path and where they will lead.

To my beautiful son, your sacrifice has been great over the period of several years, while I followed guidance to assist the world. My heart is always with you and has always been in a place of preparing for your future, by assisting in the raising of the vibration of humanity. It will soon be up to you and all like you, the torch has been lit. Bringer of Light!

To our namesake, Ganesha, with my love and gratitude for your unearthly vibration of power and gentleness in overcoming obstacles. You served us well. With your help, the extraordinary expression of a living center in Las Vegas was produced with sheer love and faith.

A precious tool one can use for spiritual expansion is to allow - space between the words – for quiet awareness

~Lee Papa & Didier Ciambra~

This book is for YOU. There is something for everyone, as there is not a single person I know who does not have a challenge to overcome in some area of their life. The purpose for sharing my intimate story is to help you find inner peace and access the tools to well-being – Mind – Body – Spirit.

The Temple of All Knowing was my labor of love for humanity. It is a vehicle, which took me 4 years to complete, to provide a source of inspiration and hope for those struggling with their life's predicaments. This memoir details my life in early 2000s, full of illness, drama and trauma, a challenged marriage, financial devastation, heartbreak as the caretaker for my elderly live-in mother and more. A life I created. And a life I transformed.

I am passionate about the message that Spirituality is not about religion and it is not "woo-woo." The energy that created all, is not discriminatory – it does not label. It does not point fingers if you have abundant money, drink alcohol, eat meat, have tattoos or smoke. Spirituality and science are bridging a gap and it is an extraordinary time to be developing and going within. Creator energy is not judgmental. You do not have to give away all your worldly possessions to be spiritual.

What this energy wants us to do is to love, to experience and gain wisdom and knowledge. And by all means...have fun.

If you have picked up this book, there is no accident. I say to my students – "Take what resonates – leave the rest."

As a previously self-proclaimed skeptic, I ask you to do the same. There are resources that we have access to for a more fulfilling life and I do not want a single person to miss them. The inspired information in this book is for everyone that is drawn to it. Everyone and anyone who is in need of healing emotional dis-ease, who want to transform their lives to more successful, joyful, peaceful and loving ones. It is for those who question their place on earth and if there is a higher power.

The book details my extraordinary near-death experience and offers the wisdom that was gained by the journey. It is for all people, not just spiritual seekers as it provides wisdom to shift your current situation to a more profound and happier state of living, personally and professionally. The experience offered me a glimpse into the encyclopedia of what it means to be alive – connecting science and spirituality in a more understandable way.

The book is encouraging, supportive and loving and will assist you in accessing YOUR Temple of All Knowing.

The story is peppered with anecdotal experiences that helps the readers know how to navigate their lives in the "Slipstream" with ease and grace.

You will come to understand the brilliant clues that are left like breadcrumbs, to guide you on your path to their destiny.

INTRODUCTION

I slept and I dreamed that life is all joy. I woke and I saw that life is all service. I served and I saw that service is joy

~Kahlil Gibran~

When you are whirling in the middle of despair amidst personal and/or professional ruin, it is hard to believe that there is light at the end of the tunnel. Often, we pray for help or return back to past religious connections to reach in and grab us out of the hole of desperation. My hope is that, through this book, this story will inspire you to the understanding that there is divine greatness at work every moment of every day and that the light that we seek at the end of that tunnel is, in fact, closer than we think – it is within each of us.

My life was like so many, overburdened with responsibility and no vibrancy as I was bogged down with negative self-talk and victimization. Through a near-death experience, I was able to return to a place that is more like home than this world, that touched me in a way that I had not even known to dream about.

Take this journey with me, you might see for yourself.

CHAPTER 1   THE PHONE CALL

All things that truly matter – beauty, love, creativity, joy, inner-peace – arise from beyond the mind

~Eckhart Tolle~

The phone rang; it was Delphine. It was a Sunday afternoon early 2008. I took the call and moved to the denim-covered glider that was in my 3-year old son's room to have the conversation.

My sister calling was not odd, but she opened with "Can you talk? I have an urgent message from Aunt Beatrice."

My sister practices meditation in which she regularly communicates with Spirit beings and our dead relatives. In everyday conversation, Delphine would mention things like, "I spoke to Dad or Uncle John ..." (both had passed), and relate a story or an emotional healing process she went through while receiving the communication. I thought this was amazing and believed in the possibility, when Delphine, or De for short, would discuss this other worldly messaging.

I would find myself having an internal dialogue debating if she was actually making this connection or was she delusional. When she would speak of something that she "received" from the Spirit world, and I would come to realize she could not have otherwise known, a fleeting twinge of jealousy peaked in the window of my subconscious. Could she really be speaking with Dad and Aunt Bea? And if she is, how come SHE is the one with this ability? I was not proud of it, but I was most definitely questioning the decision of the Universe to have Delphine be the messenger of heaven.

My sister was not the one of the three of us girls whom you would consider to be the "good" one or the most religious growing up, but actually to the contrary. She would have been described as the Bull in the China Shop by my mother, as the one most apt to finger point or cause trouble. Sophia, the eldest, had the first born light shining upon her by my mother and father, even though, she was what some would consider a problem child for she pushed the envelope of life in so many ways. Her antics included jumping out of the 2nd story building of our private high school to skipping class and developing the first female tackle football team in her teenage years, to much more complicated and explorative behaviors that provided my parents with reasons to call on prayer and saintly assistance.

Delphine was the quiet one as the middle child of our youth, until she found her voice later in her teens. She was often over-shadowed by the exuberance and manipulation of Sophia when she was being used as a co-conspirator for our eldest sister's secretive escapades of the 1970s. When I came around, my role of the "baby of the family" was not always appreciated by my older sisters, and as I matured, the less they liked this pedestal I was propped up on as "the good one."

How is she doing it? I thought. How is De getting these messages from Aunt Bea?

My elderly Aunt Bea had died more than 10 years earlier while in the presence of my mother, my sister, Delphine, one of my older female cousins, and me in the living room of our family home. I had lived in that house from the time I was born until I got married to my first husband, Anthony, at age 20.

Our house was a 3 bedroom, middle class row home in Baltimore City, Maryland. The 12 by 12 foot front room, where I grew up and where we watched TV programs on the console television that offered just three major stations for your viewing enjoyment. Although the room was small, when we were little and the family piled in to watch Sonny & Cher, it felt huge. As the entry room to our family home, I experienced most of my fond memories there. This is where we opened our Christmas gifts under our decorated 5-foot Frasier fir tree that stood seemingly tall, as if it could reach the stars on a wooden platform, to set the stage for this holiday focal point. In reality, the Christmas tree was no taller than the height I currently stand.

Christmas was a very special time in our Catholic family. Not overly religious, mind you, but the whole Santa Clause phenomenon was beautifully orchestrated with all the mystery and wonder that a child could hope to receive. The Christmas tree was secretly stored in the basement well of the stairs until we kids were all asleep and then my parents would work through the night to make a spectacular show of lights and hand-wrapped presents from old paper bags and twine adorned with our names scribbled on by "elves." This was a tradition handed down from my mother's family who grew up during the depression and fancy wrapping paper was a luxury. Christmas was magical!

After my parents would signal that Santa had indeed arrived, my sister Sophia and I would rush down the stairs to witness the light show of the tree, and we would tear through our presents leaving no time for individual gift lingering. Delphine, on the other hand, was not so quick; instead, she would slowly and methodically use her scissors to gently unwrap each gift with all the appreciation of an unwrapped Tiffany blue box that none of us had ever experienced. Later as we became adults, Delphine would prop herself preciously on the couch, and while filing her nails, would direct me to the spots on the tree that were missing lights and Christmas balls.

This is the same living room where my nature-loving father would let our hamster out of the cage while directing us three children to lie on the floor and make a circular barrier with our arms. That little chubby, furry rodent was a family pet, and we loved him. My dad loved animals, so we had a bunch of them from Dutch rabbits, to hamsters, cats, and frogs - but never a dog. My mother was afraid of dogs. The hamster outing was strategically orchestrated during the time of my mother's weekly visit to the Farmers Market in downtown Baltimore across from the corner row house where she grew up, and where several of her sisters still lived. Mom would not have tolerated such nonsense and activity on her prized oriental rug. This was the room where my Aunt Bea allowed me to lie down on the sofa when I was a child, and she would stroke my head and rub my back until I would fall asleep. She had such a loving and confident manner. I always felt safe with her.

My mother's side of the family was the most involved and influential in our lives, especially Aunt Bea. She was the family matriarch, our lifeline and leader. She was loving, intelligent, strong, certainly had her opinions, some may say controlling ones, but if it weren't for her emotional and financial support, we and her sisters' and brother's families would not have had as many essentials provided for and certainly not any niceties.

She was a savvy businesswoman, so deferring to her made sense. For her era, Aunt Bea was super cool and open minded, rising to heights in her profession at C&P Telephone Company when women were just starting to be acknowledged in the workforce. She was a petite woman with an incredible sense of style and pep in her step that oozed confidence and excitement for the possibilities of life. It also made it difficult to walk with her as she was down the block before you had taken your first step. Aunt Bea never married, but made her siblings' families her own. Sometimes the involvement would have been considered today as "too much." There is usually a price to pay when you are being rescued. But I loved her and I thought she was amazing, just as my mother did. Aunt Bea was my mother's best friend.

Aunt Bea believed in reincarnation before it was an accepted concept to consider openly, as this was the 1950s and 60s when my sisters and I were born. We were raised in a devout Catholic family, and such things were not dinner topics, nor was it on our radar at that time.

As easily as it was for me to pull up these cherished memories, it was the hope and promise that communication could continue from beyond death.

There was something about witnessing the passing of my cherished aunt in my family living room, with all the whispered memories of the past that seemed oddly normal. Not that this sort of thing ever happened before or since, in my presence or in my home, but there was a natural feeling about it. We are born, we live, and then we die.

I found the manner of those surrounding this process akin to a physiological experiment of human nature. It is fascinating how people react around those who are dying. Different personality types react differently as, of course, they would, but to experience it firsthand was somewhat of an emotional study. There are some who see this as a sacred space and whisper and dote on the laboring body. Yet, there are those who manage stressful situations by joking and laughing and breaking the somber atmosphere with quips. There are those who embellish their role in the caretaking and the history and relationship with the dying to make it more impactful. And as days, weeks, years pass, the story may change - just as the recollection of this experience for me, many years later holds a different value than that of the immediate experience.

The final stages of the passing of a loved one, in the physical state that my aunt was in can take any length of time. She was elderly. My mother's mother and those of her sisters and brother who had died were in their 80s and 90s. Our family not only has great genes, but growing up I was surrounded by holistic methods to wellness.

Vitamins, Cod Liver Oil and Apple Cider Vinegar were staples in our house growing up. You would have never found a soda pop or sugar cereal for miles around our family. Although as children, we felt like oddballs, our parents did us a great service.

Now as a witness to the process of my aunt's decline, I found it difficult as she had been such a healthy, vital woman for so long. The caretaking of this shadow of the once vibrant being took a physical and emotional toll on my mother and others assisting, which is understandable, especially when you have no idea when the process will stop. I suspect an internal war of guilt can arise from those caring for the dying. Being in the pre-mourning stage with a loved one in their final days can be an extraordinary example of loving service, and yet, over time, the feeling of exhaustion and emotional weight is begging to be released by the passing of the individual. I wonder what the person dying is feeling or thinking?

My role was small. I was not there a lot, managing my young marriage and a full-time job, but what I do remember is a feeling that my aunt was just getting through the process of allowing her body to let go. Many times the family caretakers and visitors were in the kitchen speaking loudly and often exuberantly laughing and joking, only 2 rooms away, but in a small row house this is easily just 15 steps. One time, it apparently annoyed my fading aunt to the degree that she yelled out for them to stop, with enough force to be heard. This had been surprising for one so physically weak that it startled us. Although, in line with her personality, her willpower was strong and she wanted to be acknowledged. She got her point across.

As my mother, Delphine, and I surrounded the hospital bed, each of us had our hands on Aunt Bea as a way to comfort her. As I previously noted, Mom and Aunt Bea were best friends, and this was very hard for my already aging mother. Mom was close on the left side of her so that she could whisper lovingly, and my sister and I were on the right of her holding her hand as she labored and struggled to release her body. The rattling got worse, and the emotion in all of us began to seep up as Aunt Bea took her last breath letting out a sigh that told us she was gone.

Being in the presence of someone taking their last breath of life is a very intimate and precious experience to be allowed to share. I realize this as I have gotten older and feel honored by my aunt for allowing it. I think this is why many dying people wait for their loved ones, who hold vigil over their passing body, to take a potty break or retire for the evening to transition and release their physical vehicle in private.

"Did you hear me?" Delphine pulled me back to the present.

As I return to my sister's phone call, it was out of the ordinary that Delphine began with, "Can you talk?" Typically my sister doesn't wait past the first syllables of hello before she enthusiastically starts her end of the conversation, that quiet contemplative child had transformed into the Lioness of her zodiac sign. But this time was different.

"I have an urgent message for you!" she said. Once again, this is not the typical conversation starter.

I pulled myself back to the conversation and responded reluctantly, "Okay, what is it?"

I love my sister who is three years my senior, although we have not always been close. Actually, more often than not, we are not talking. We go through short periods of understanding and communication and then falling out and not speaking for long periods of time. This is mostly associated with old wounds that cannot get healed - an intolerance of the differences in personality and what we choose to focus our attentions on. We mostly have different perspectives on the same situation, and are mostly intolerant of each other's perspectives.

My family has always thrived on drama and trauma. It is almost as if there are another set of veins running through us that feed off of the drama as a way to thrive. Although we have discussed the "need of drama" amongst ourselves and, try as we might to push it away, it rears its ugly presence more often than not. Just like with everyone, it all boils down to our perceptions. Two people involved in a situation, yet there are two ways to view it.

During this stage of acceptance, we were in communication and almost at a level of appreciation for each other's idiosyncrasies and unique oddities as something to be celebrated. Okay, I said almost! We did have the same sense of humor. When one of us got the other going, there were most definitely forthcoming tears of laughter. This annoyed my mother at times because it felt like a private joke but, in fact, it was not private at all, it was just silliness. I love that about my sister.

"I was speaking with Aunt Bea ..." Delphine interrupted my thoughts, "Aunt Bea told me that you need to slowww down and take care of yourself, or you are headed for a big fall."

A "Big Fall" was emphasized. I have no idea if Delphine was embellishing here, as Whoopi Goldberg's character stressed in Ghost when speaking to Demi Moore's character: ("Molly, you in danger, girl!) Or was De quoting my aunt directly?

CHAPTER 2   THE MOVE

Take the first step in faith. You don't have to see the whole staircase. Just take the first step
~Dr. Martin Luther King, Jr~

My response was immediate and knee-jerk.

"I don't know how I am supposed to slow down when I have a young child, an 80-year-old mother to care for, and a husband who is dealing with the physical and emotional effects of a car accident."

There was more: "Delphine, we are in over our heads here with this real estate business crashing in on us. We are possibly losing our house because we cannot continue to pay this exorbitant mortgage anymore."

"I know you understand," I told De, as she was in the same position with her house. "But I worry how our situation is going to impact Mom."

We had moved her into our home 4 years prior, and now the market was plummeting. I was not sure she could handle another big disruption. My mother was strong and physically very healthy, yet to talk to her you would have thought she was on her death bed. It was easy for anyone not understanding the dynamics to get pulled into this self-evoked suffering as reality.

I continued, "She thought she would be here for the rest of her days, and so did we." I took a breath and continued, "I am trying to keep my business alive, too. On top of all that, we have the impending lawsuit for Jean-Pierre's accident. Listen, Delphine, any one of these problems would be stressful, but I am juggling more than my fair share here. I'm drowning, and I see no lifeline." In short, a Big Fall seemed like an extremely good bet.

The emotional and financial pressures were mounting by the minute. My husband, Jean-Pierre and I were married in Los Angeles in 2002. We lived in a small, sweet rental house in Hollywood that was just big enough for us and our cats, but not for my mother too. After Mom's devastating fall that broke her hip while she was alone at home and took her 45 minutes to crawl to the phone, the dialogue began about her living with us.

It took some convincing over a period of months, but as Mom knew herself, she was having more and more difficulty driving and managing the responsibilities of her house. She was not eating properly unless you think hot dogs account for several food groups. She was extremely lonely and showing signs of depression. We wanted to offer her an incredible next chapter of her life, free from worry and responsibility. We had no doubt that mom would flourish with us. How could she not?

It had been Jean-Pierre's idea, one of a loving European family man, to suggest such an arrangement. There was not a viable option with my other siblings and we thought the best solution was to make the move while Mom was still part of the decision process.

While exploring possible places for a potential move to accommodate Mom, we looked at cities in Idaho and Utah, amongst others. Our friend Jane mentioned that Nevada was booming and we should consider it. We both made a face with a gesture of an unpleasing consideration.

"By the way, there is no state income tax." Jane mentioned.

"We're moving to Las Vegas!" Jean Pierre exclaimed.

We found our beautiful new house in Las Vegas in 2003, not knowing that we bought near the top of the real estate market. We moved, thinking as entrepreneurs, and we decided to launch new careers as real estate professionals which would give us the time flexibility needed to care for Mom. We were extremely optimistic about our future and, contrary to the stereotypes of this place, we knew we were going to like living here. There was a buzz.

All I previously knew about Las Vegas was stuff I didn't like. I had visited several times for varied reasons, mostly work-related. There was too much stimulation for my taste: the bells, the lights, and the over indulgence. I didn't "get" Vegas, but now we were here to live and we found out it was all new! And clean! It was exhilarating being a part of a growing city.

There were new shops going up all the time to explore. The chatter while you were in line at the grocery was about the next new store that "we were getting."

"Did you hear a new Trader Joes is coming to Henderson?"

"No!" "Where?" "When?"

I loved the idea of the weather, as I do not enjoy the cold. I never understood why people in L.A. had pools. It was never warm enough for me to get in them. I like it hot!

We were getting ready to understand what living in the desert meant. We were told the average daily temperature was 66 degrees, which sounded wonderful, but in the summer, it can reach upwards of 120 degrees Fahrenheit.

"It's dry heat," people would say. Ha! Yeah, it's dry and extremely hot. Well, it used to be dry, but with the influx of so many homes, lawns, water features, and pools, there now was some humidity. The winters are mild, we would hear, and that was extremely appealing, too. Of course, our first winter it snowed. The best part of that is it was all melted in a day. Weird climate to some and amazing for me.

We felt so good about our move to this exciting developing city, and prepared for the arrival of my mother to come and live with us in our beautiful new home that was chosen for her needs. Mom or Ellie, the name which is short for Elaine, is what we would call her from time to time - not out of disrespect, but rather out of a more informal, loving friendship, and she loved it. Anything that made her feel special would make her beam. It was so wonderful to experience her in this manner that we tried extremely hard to nurture this reaction.

I had idolized my mother all my life. I was her biggest fan, cheerleader, and protector. We were two peas in a pod. We looked alike, and we had the same taste in material goods from clothes to household items. We liked to do the same things. We laughed at the same jokes and had the same sense of humor. She was my buddy and my best friend. The relationship, even into adulthood, was extremely close. She was my confidante, and she loved that.

We were like school girls who keep secrets. Mom would fly from Baltimore to visit me in Los Angeles from time to time, and I always made it spectacular for her. She was my main focus whenever she was present. I drenched her with love and attention. It was easy; it was fun. She drank it up like a thirsty camel.

Mom adored Jean-Pierre and she loved the male attention. We had the flexibility to be with her because we worked from home. We provided a stable and loving environment that was drama free and peaceful.

The new house seemed like a dream come true, especially when compared to Los Angeles, with so much house for the money! This would offer us the amount of space to live harmoniously without getting in each other's way. Twenty-five hundred square feet, all on one story, dual master bedrooms, four bedrooms in all, three bathrooms, a central great-room, a three-car garage, and lush landscaping – even in the desert. Here, Mom would have her own suite, including a large bedroom area and private bath and walk-in closet. Her bedroom was huge and brightly lit by the main large window from the front of the house. Interestingly, the way the house was laid out, this was the only window from the front offering her a view of our private cul-de-sac and the fabulous weeping tree. In comparison, the rest of the house was quite dark.

A mix of her old furniture and newly-purchased additions rounded out her space that included a queen bed, side tables, a dresser, and a desk with a large comfortable chair. She would have privacy, quiet, abundant sunshine, and a peacefulness you could feel just walking into the house. You almost wanted to whisper. This was suburban living at its best.

I adored this house and the neighborhood. It felt new and full of promise for all of us. Jean-Pierre was not as much in love with it as I was, but we had been looking for quite a while, and everything that we had seen previously offered more challenges with respect to an in-law apartment. They all felt like an afterthought in the other homes instead of incorporation. This house arrangement provided the bones of a really great space for all of us.

Being on the end of the cul-de-sac offered peace and tranquility. We dreamed of what we would do with the enormous backyard once we had the money to expand and add landscaping; maybe even another detached building that would offer even more space for mom as a separate living room. We had lost one house that we had put an offer on, and we were running out of time. We had given notice on our rental house in L.A. It was time to jump in.

We were nervous about such a big commitment, but the market was strong, we were skilled professionals, and we were confident we would thrive. The house, which was definitely a stretch for us financially, even though Mom helped with the down payment, it offered the best option to accommodate our needs. The scary part and the nagging internal voice was that we were entrepreneurs moving to a new city with no guarantee of work, beyond the apparently endless boom in the real estate market. The concept of a house that would cost this much to a Baltimore gal growing up in a small row house was a stretch, but after being desensitized to real estate prices by living in Los Angeles, this investment seemed reasonable.

"We are hard workers and are doing the right thing by caring for my mother. What could go wrong?" I remember re-telling this advice to Jean-Pierre that I had received from an ex-employer who was a New York real estate mogul some 20 years ago.

"When buying a house," my extremely successful and well-respected employer said, "stretch and buy as much as you can because it will always go up." We stretched all right, and for the first couple of years it was not an issue.

The location was great. Based on Mom's needs and criteria we scripted, we chose well: close to shopping, a Catholic church with the same name as Mom attended in Baltimore, St. Thomas More, and access to all the services and accoutrements she desired. We bought in one of the best school districts in Vegas by accident, so when our son, Luke, came along in 2005, this location was perfect for his eventual schooling.

The real estate market was booming. Jean-Pierre and I were working together and getting established as residential and commercial Realtors® working for a local brokerage. We decided to go to real estate school almost immediately upon arriving in Vegas. With my past commercial and property management experience and Jean-Pierre's financial expertise, we thought it would be a great industry for us to launch our careers in Vegas, allowing us the flexibility to attend to Mom's needs.

We learned very quickly that every Tom, Dick, bartender and stripper (dancer) was getting a real estate license because at the time, it was perceived as a license to print money. Las Vegas had been undervalued for so long. Now that the market was moving from healthy to robust, to pregnant with greed, the feeding frenzy was palpable. We jumped in with the intention that clients would see the value in working with professionals as opposed to part-time unskilled agents.

The first cruel stab of fate - or indicator that our lives were taking a detour in the wrong direction - came in February 2004, only 2 months after our arrival to Las Vegas, and my mother had yet to arrive in her new city. The phone rang and I heard:

"Lee, it's Jean-Pierre. I am okay." Those words were the prologue to wreckage that haunts us even today.

"What happened? Are you okay? Where are you?"

I was stammering. My heart was racing. I could hear my heart beat in my head. The anxiety was welling up in me as he recounted, too slowly for my liking, what had just taken place about three miles from our home. Jean-Pierre had been stopped at an intersection waiting for the red light to turn green when a white truck came barreling into him from behind at significant speed.

"It was a good thing I was in your car because it is solid," Jean-Pierre said. "I am sorry. The car - it's finished, I'm afraid."

I had a pang of nostalgia for my champagne-colored vintage BMW 325i convertible that I had bought in Los Angeles from a friend's dad. It was in amazing shape, and I adored that car.

Jean-Pierre sounded strange. "Don't worry about the car. What happened?" I asked. "Are you hurt?" I added.

"I don't know," he replied. "The truck never stopped, until it hit me. I saw him coming in my rear view mirror, but I had nowhere to go, so I just braced myself."

A blip in time. A moment that happens that changes the trajectory of your entire life. This gentle, easygoing, fit, healthy, loving man changed in that split moment. Chronic pain, resulting from spinal and neck injury, stopped him where he stood. Literally. He could barely walk anymore.

I thought about the struggle that Jean-Pierre had over the past several years. When I had met him in Los Angeles in May of 2001, he was just downsizing a business that was his big dream: a revolutionary software company that was going to change the world and make a difference. His entire heart and soul had been his business, and failing was not an option. Even when he was making the final move from his high-end office space on Wilshire Blvd. to a home office, after the last of the employees had been let go, he still had hope. Then, 9-11 occurred and the world began mourning and everyone was changed.

The world has lived through massive catastrophe before and, although altered and imprinted with the energy of the occurrence, life finds a way of brushing off the rubble to move on. I was going to love him enough and support him enough to get through this. How did the bad luck follow us to the desert?

At least real estate was still booming, but with Jean-Pierre's fractured body and spirit, working at capacity was not in the cards. Mom moved in with us in June 2004, and by New Year's Eve, we were pregnant. This was miraculous as we had tried for more than a year to get pregnant, including fertility assistance, and nothing. We had released the idea and any medical intervention before the holidays to give us a break and surrendered to the idea that it might not be in the plan for us. I thought the stress of the accident, thus the strain on our relationship due to the chronic pain and the lawsuit and the managing of Mom settling in with us, probably wasn't the best incubator for a healthy baby.

I never had a weight problem, but this pregnancy gave me the free pass to eat whatever I wanted, and I did. I was not feeding an urge or a craving; I was feeding my unhappiness with everything else in my life, but my baby. I enjoyed Baskin Robbins ice cream on a daily basis, gaining 65 pounds when I was at full term. Ahhh, Jamoca Almond Fudge. Can you say, "Love on a cone!"

Late in my pregnancy, I sat in front of my computer one morning before sunrise as I had trouble sleeping in my last trimester. Difficult for a sleep lover. Seriously, 9 hours is a good night. What could be better than sleep? So, one morning, I waddled into the bedroom-turned-shared-office for both Jean-Pierre and me and decided it was time to name our child. We had not decided on a name that we both were really jazzed about.

I got shot down on the name Gabrielle because during my pregnancy, after a steamy dream, I had a "thing" for the Irish actor Gabriel Byrne, and Jean-Pierre was not on board. So, I consciously tapped into my baby explaining that if he had any input in the naming process, now was the time. I scanned Italian and French boy's names on the internet and, as my eyes rolled past several possibilities, I jotted them down. I looked at the meanings of the names as well, and when I saw the one name in particular that made my heart leap, I knew I had found it.

I picked two others and made a note as a game for Jean-Pierre to have an opportunity to experience the KNOWING that I did. It was a beautiful, soulful connection, and that morning our son was named Luke, meaning "Bringer of Light." Our son, Luke, was born almost at the crest of that crazy real estate market. Oh, what an amazing little being.

My friend, Jane, who never had children joked, "I wonder if parents can tell if their child is ugly, or is there some brain chemical that makes them think their child is beautiful so they love it?"

I was in hysterics with the honesty as I had never contemplated this, and, yet, it seemed to make sense. Of course our child is beautiful!!! He is healthy, which seems especially precious, since we had him after trying for so long. I still vividly remember my pregnancy and nurturing the growing miracle in my belly. I was 42 years old when our son was born - the same age my mother was when she had me. My mother's birthday fell on the 19th day of March, mine was the 19th day of September, and now our little angel was the 9th day of September. This seemed to offer an interesting coincidence that my life was mimicking that of my mother in this way.

Jean-Pierre had to get back to work. We both did, as I had taken a lot of time with Mom gently making the adjustment to her new living situation. I took five months off work to focus on nurturing our new baby and navigating the most natural and scary thing in this new mother's life…breast-feeding. I could start and close companies, I could hire and fire employees, I could navigate power lunches, I could raise money and steer my way through business obstacles, but breast feeding, the most natural thing in the world, eluded me.

I cried and cried: "I can't feed my baby." When I was in the hospital, after 30-plus hours of labor and a C-Section (bless my Plastic Surgeon turned Obstetrician for the meticulous sew job) and my nurse who I dubbed the Lactating Nazi put the fear of Mother Earth in me to make sure that I breast-fed.

The mounting pressure was getting to me. "I can do this." I sought help from the local outreach hospital for guidance. It turned out there is this miracle herb called Fenugreek that brings in breast milk. Who knew? Adding a breast pump to the equation and just relaxing did the trick. My mother helped a lot. She was needed, and that is what SHE needed. We did it! I did it!

Jean-Pierre was incredible with Luke. He was such a proud father. I took the lead on the baby stuff, as mothers mostly do, and as a control freak Virgo would have to do, but it worked. We shared the experience always, mostly Jean-Pierre behind the camera documenting the best thing in our lives. Motherhood changed me. And I am sure it had to do with the hormones, too, but nothing else mattered but this baby. Now I was part of a club called mothers. When any child, and I mean ANY child, was crying or in distress, something viscerally welled up in me and I had to stop the urge to run to that child. This includes children on television commercials!

Jean-Pierre was happy with his role as father and there were glimmers of playfulness that would shine through in between the internal suffering he was experiencing due to his accident. One day early in the breast-feeding drama, Jean-Pierre was walking through the living room to get to the bedroom as I was organized on the couch. With no other exchange, I heard him voice…"Mmmoooo" as a commentary to my breast-pumping. I adored his humor, and that is probably the trait that I loved most about him when we were newly navigating our relationship. My once playful husband was still there somewhere and he would show himself briefly, but for the most part, that quality of him was absent.

This should have been a very intimate time for us and there were moments, but living in a house with another adult, especially an elderly relative, adds a layer of complexity and lack of privacy. Jean-Pierre and I were managing, but that was it. Managing.

Mom was an incredible support, though. As we spent more and more time together, I understood this need of hers to be needed, but there was something else developing that was unnerving. She would stand just on the periphery of what was going on. We would have to continually ask her to join in. It was a kind of lurking in the background. Being too conscious and fearful of being in the way made for an unnatural and uncomfortable exchange.

Even though we had these issues with Jean-Pierre's chronic pain and Mom's outward vibe of being uncomfortable, for the most part, we could allow all that to go and have times of joy, but not for long. The real estate market, and our livelihood, was in peril and was started to act like a runaway train. Buyers, at this time, could not make offers quick enough, and sellers were overzealous with what their property was worth. There was unscrupulous business and financial activity going on all around.

When a property is worth what a buyer is willing to pay, and the buyers are drunk with a manipulated market, you can see how there is no place else for this story to go but down, and we were in the middle of it.

We were professional, ethical, and customer service oriented. That was not always appreciated when there were so many unprincipled dealings going on that led to massive financial rewards for some, and jail for others, as the deck of cards began to fall. Long before the national banking crisis of 2008, fear was spreading like a cancer through the Las Vegas Valley, and you could smell it, feel it, and taste it.

Some were frenzied with trying to make deals before the bubble burst, but for us the urgency to make enough money each month to cover our ridiculous monthly mortgage started to become paralyzing. Jean-Pierre and I were feeling the shroud of failure, embarrassment, humiliation, and shame as it was becoming clear that we were going to be victims of a real estate market collapse – and no one but us had held our feet to the fire to be involved.

By the time Delphine and I had our telephone conversation, this reality was practically suffocating me.

"It would be lovely to take Aunt Bea's advice and just slow down, Delphine, but that is not possible. I have too much responsibility and obligation here. There is nothing I can give up."

"Don't shoot the messenger!" was Delphine's reply.

CHAPTER 3   THE TRUTH

Rivers know this -
There is no hurry. We shall get there some day
                              ~Winnie the Pooh~

Delphine was right. I was taking my extreme frustration about my current situation and my spiraling fears out on my sister, or worse, on the spirit of my deceased aunt, who was apparently trying to help by communicating through a psychic channel. I was not 100 percent committed to the belief that my sister was indeed talking to my aunt, but I was not prepared to doubt it, either. I believed that certain people had the gift to speak to the other side, and I knew my sister was working full-time on meditation and taking classes to expand her channel. So, had she really acquired this gift? I certainly had the door open to the possibility. Delphine and I said cordial goodbyes, and I thanked her for the message.

After hanging up the phone, I continued the dialogue in my thoughts while gliding in the chair, reviewing the past few years that brought me to this predicament. The house. Our jobs. Our marriage. My mother. In a mere five years, everything had changed. With more bills to pay, and less money coming in every month, I felt like I was driving that runaway train. But it wasn't just about money. Jean-Pierre was in pain, depressed, and our marriage was becoming more and more a shadow of a once beautiful union. My mother was hiding in her room more and more. And Delphine was right: I was constantly sick, maybe seriously so. The family that once seemed perfect now took on an increasingly fractured dynamic.

This would be the ultimate scenario for my family back East to rally around the drama at my funeral. I could hear it now, "Oh, poor Lee, blah blah blah, and Ellie…she should have never moved to Las Vegas…You know that was the beginning of the end…blah blah blah." Just another juicy nut of drama for the family to get a hold of, to chew on.

Jean-Pierre had gained 70lbs since the car accident. He became angry, short-tempered, and disheartened. He walked with an adjusted gate, leaning toward one side and his neck at an angle. The subsequent lawsuit, which took four years to conclude, solidified his pain and the anguish day after day, as he was forced to keep a journal of all his pain and disability and how it affected his daily life. Page after page after page of detail reinforced his debilitating accident.

He became a shell of the man he used to be, lost in the fiber of one disabled. There were glimpses of the old Jean-Pierre, and that was my salvation. I waited for the spark and the twinkle in his eyes to return while walking on eggshells and searching for answers everywhere to ease his pain. I prayed for guidance and direction. I was going to find an answer for this man. I was going to fix it, because that is what I do. I am a researcher and I am a finder and I am a fixer. If there was a holistic approach to this problem, I was going to uncover it because what he was doing thus far wasn't working.

Meanwhile, Jean-Pierre followed his doctors' and lawyers' orders. Appointments with a pain management specialist, physical therapy, prescriptions, MRI's, surgeons, more pain management doctors, second and third opinions in Las Vegas and Los Angeles, more prescriptions, and finally, surgery as the last result. He was at his end, and the downward spiral didn't end there.

Jean-Pierre developed pneumonia from being in the hospital, and my frantic call to the doctor when I thought he was dying, led me to assist this 250-pound man to the car and rushing him to the UMC emergency room. The prognosis was touch and go. I sat on the phone with the attending doctor at the hospital for an hour that evening, as Luke and Mom needed my attention at home. I was torn between two locations.

The doctor prepared me for the possibility of the drugs not working and that Jean-Pierre might not make it. I was not giving up on him, as I was sobbing on the phone. "He is strong. He was never sick in his life until Vegas," I told the doctor. "Why was this happening to us? How can I fix this?" I thought, as I continued to cry after ending the communication with the doctor.

Given Jean-Pierre's strong constitution, he slowly recovered from this trauma, and recuperated from home after a long term hospital stay, but due to the massive doses of steroids that had to be used to save him, the residual effects led to excruciating pain in his joints.

As my husband suffered from his severe injury and bout with pneumonia, my mother seemed to be performing a strange vanishing act before our very eyes. When she moved in, I had taken several months off work to help her get adjusted in Las Vegas. She would no longer be driving, since she was legally blind in one eye and it would have been irresponsible to allow it, even though she wanted to.

When she learned she would have to take the DMV test, she quickly agreed – no more driving.

I explored a mini bus sponsored by the city to pick her up and take her places, and worked out getting discount coupons for taxi cab service. I found her a nearby hairdresser, and we would spend time doing errands and just being together. Of course, there would be an adjustment. My mother lived in the same house for over 40 years. She no longer went to the same church, had the same friends and family near her, the same post office, or the same restaurants. I was conscious of how difficult this must be, and I tried to soothe her fears.

When she lived in Baltimore, she complained daily to me over the phone about her life, so I wanted to make sure she had an opportunity to develop her new life. She wanted independence, too, so there was a juggling act of allowing her to have her space and involving her in our lives. The senior discount coupons for taxis would give her additional freedom to get around. Jean-Pierre and I were also available to drive her to the hairdresser or church and we would rotate our schedules to accommodate her. But as years went by, she slowed down her outings and spent more time in her room; increasingly glued to the television, especially Fox News and Sean Hannity, which was not what I expected. But I came to realize this was the nucleus of my mother's life view.

We tried to include Mom in our social activities, time and time again asking her to join us, and going through a ritual of cajoling and coaxing, most of the time she would just sequester herself in her room. I had to admit, none of us were now comfortable with the living arrangement. But we had made a commitment, and we were going to make it work. Mom would act apologetic, as if she were disturbing us, and it became increasingly harder to pull her in. The environment was emotionally ill. I grew weary of the game of inviting her to social events or even to the living room to be with us, only for her to say no in a manner that oozed manipulation. The effort was weighty. Who was this woman? The truth was I really didn't know her.

I began to realize that the person I had built up in my mind, and with whom I had actively participated all these years, was not the person I was living with now. That other mother was my subjective reality, not some absolute reality. I now saw that she had carved out a portion of her personality that was just for me, and I had fed it. I nurtured it and even helped form it. I learned that no one was exempt from my mother's complaining or judgment, although still not realizing that I was also on the menu of her complaints. The long list of doctor visits to address Mom's physical complaints was exhausting proof of her negativity.

My mother was made comfortable by a negative spin on life, and I had participated with her in her reality since childhood, pacifying her while she complained about people around her and any situation that may come her way. Yet, the glimmers of joy were precious. When she was happy, she beamed with the radiance of angels, and the energy that emanated from her was beautiful and intoxicating. I loved that part of her, and I waited for those moments, those hours, those days to get me through. They became fewer.

Now I realized that my mother's need for constant attention was sucking the life straight from my being. I cried over the disappointment of not meeting my expectations of being a good enough daughter and making Mom happy. I struggled at the core of my soul with what I could be doing differently for all of us to have a better life. I believed the decision to move Mom in with us had been the right one; we made the decision from the heart. But what went wrong?

Mom's incessant complaining and regurgitating of Fox News stories that were retelling the misery of the world with a propaganda spin that was just drama churning, was seriously affecting me. Layer that on top of Jean-Pierre's European-style passion for any intellectually spawned debate: periodically, sparks flew in a heated discussion in this now contentious household.

Jean-Pierre and I had lived in Los Angeles for years, and our political and religious views are a match. We leave room for possibility and additional views for our own expansion, but we have moved beyond the doctrine of religion and are core spiritual people. Mom understood that about me and seemed to be okay with my spiritual beliefs, not political views, and so I would attend Sunday mass with her as I knew she liked it, and the ritual of mass was somehow calming. We had basically had a peaceful life prior to moving to Las Vegas. We believe in Mother Earth and the amazing gifts she has to offer. I believed in a God somewhere out there that would assist if asked.

We were thrilled when President Obama got into office during his first term and rocked the world. We both cried in joy. However, my mother said the rosary.

My impossible role in the family dynamics was as the self-appointed peacemaker, the one who was supposed to keep everyone happy. On top of everything else, I had split away from doing real estate with Jean-Pierre to start a new business-to-business company for online trade magazines, focusing on real estate related businesses.

I thought giving Jean-Pierre and I some distance would be healthy. I was feeling an enormous amount of pressure to make this new business a viable entity. Mom always supported and believed in my professional abilities and for the most part, I had been very successful in my careers. If my job became challenging, Mom offered emotional encouragement. As I moved into entrepreneurial efforts, she would occasionally offer financial support as well, believing I just needed a break, and it was always appreciated.

I had spoiled her all my adult life, and it was hard to be in a place of receiving from her, but that in itself was a lesson. We had a mutual bond that was incredibly special when it was in sync. It was like a teeter-totter. When one was up the other was down, and we were masters at shifting the other to a higher place.

However, as time was going by, it was becoming more difficult to manage the shifting for each other. As my desire to please her and make her proud of me was met with more challenges, our situation worsened and there were increasingly more disjointed days mixed in with the peaceful, fun days. I felt that my responsibilities to everyone were more than I could manage.

"I am going to make this company work, even if it kills me," I would regularly state.

"This business cannot fail. There are too many people counting on me who have invested in me, both family, and friends."

For sure, our external circumstances were desperate. But as I sat there thinking in my son's bedroom, I was awakening to another truth. It was time for me to hold the mirror up to myself and look within in search of a path out of this darkness. Eerily, again I could see how I had mimicked my mother's life, in a way, with enormous challenges, marrying and having children late in life, living in lack, feeling the weight of the world on my shoulders as I took on personal responsibility and obligation beyond limits, and constantly looked outside myself for answers.

It seemed I had no personal time for looking within even if I wanted to. But did I really want to see?

I certainly never made time to quiet myself or even love myself for that matter. I was the insecure offspring of a self-doubting mother. Looking at the world and everyone in it as being separate from me, I tried so hard to keep control as a way to keep it all together in a mad world of my own making.

"What were the roads I took that brought me to this place of overwhelming obligation? Should we have stayed in Los Angeles? Was Jean-Pierre too heartbroken over the loss of his business there to recover? Was Jean-Pierre sorry we married and moved to suburbia when he always thrived in a city?

Who was this woman I called Mom, and how could she be so different from the mother I thought she was all my life? Will she ever be happy? Can I make her happy? Am I letting everyone down? If I try harder and push forward, can I make this all work? If I can make the business succeed, and I am bringing in good money, everyone will relax more and it will be better."

My mind was all over the place as I sat and examined my life: A 44-year-old Baltimore girl by way of Los Angeles finds herself in Sin City with a husband, a three-year-old son, an 85-year-old mother, 2 cats, a business that is failing amid the economic meltdown of Las Vegas, a husband who no longer felt like the man she married since being severely injured in the car accident, and the increasingly real threat of losing her house to foreclosure. Failure was abundant. As our stability began to crumble, I found myself tapping into the wisdom I obtained from many years of self-improvement practices at various stages of my life.

"You poor thing," my mother and other relatives would say as their instant reaction to any perceived struggle. Now I realized I was seeing myself as the victim. It was time to stop that and stop participating in the family drama authored by me, through my mother and Jean-Pierre, through me. My life and house used to be peaceful. What happened?

CHAPTER 4   THE PRAYER

The present moment is all you ever have

~Eckhart Tolle~

I returned from my contemplation in Luke's room hungry for solutions and even some magic mystical pill to make it all better. But, of course, what I found was life just where I had left off. Jean-Pierre was in the kitchen washing dishes, and Luke was playing in the great room with his cars. The television was on with a kid's movie, The Koala Brothers.

"Can you check on your mother?" Jean-Pierre asked. "I think she has fallen asleep again in her chair. That worries me," he continued. "She is going to fall out of that chair one day." I loved that about him - his concern for Mom.

I went in to Mom's room to find exactly that; her head had dropped down, and she was sitting in her chair asleep with the television program continuing on not minding that she was asleep. I gently woke her and walked her to the bed and told her to nap before dinner was ready. I kissed my mom, and she smiled and groggily agreed to nap. In that moment, I tapped into the immense love that I had for my mother and the woman I had always known.

A memory welling up of one of the first experiences imprinted in my mind and heart was of her rocking me to sleep and singing a lullaby. My mother had a very special, raspy, soft voice due to a botched vocal cord surgery many years prior. When she sang to me, the memory held a feeling of sadness and deep love that is hard to explain.

"You were right. Mom is asleep," I told Jean-Pierre. "I am going to start dinner."

As I passed Jean-Pierre walking out of the kitchen, he added: "I have a migraine coming. I am going to bed."

"Great," I sarcastically thought. "Okay, Honey," I said.

There it was; the face of one of the monsters in our house. As I knew all too well, when a migraine headache was coming, I would lose Jean-Pierre for hours or days. We had tried to figure out what triggered them since we have been together, but we never had, and so there were periods when they were frequent and there were periods when there were none. I had migraines and cluster headaches when I was in my late teens and early 20s and then into my thirties.

So, I get that they are debilitating and excruciating. When I had mine, I learned that they came when I had an internal emotional struggle. My migraines ended when I worked on self-improvement and went into therapy counseling. I offered this insight to Jean-Pierre long ago, saying that often ongoing headaches have a root cause in the emotional.

He said what he normally says when I offered something, "No," then added, "It is from a Rugby accident."

As I prepared dinner and watched Luke from the kitchen playing on the floor, I felt resentment at all the times Jean-Pierre had a migraine and I lost him. I know how incapacitating it is. It is horrible, and you do not wish that on anyone. But, I was feeling impatient.

I wanted solutions to our problems! I was more resentful that Jean-Pierre would not consider another approach besides his migraine medicine, which usually consisted of a large dose of some over-the-counter pills.

I thought I had released drama from my life long ago. I went through years of therapy and self-discovery to find out why I had so many dramas in my life. As an adult child of an alcoholic father, I learned that we find comfort in this continual feeling of walking on eggshells and waiting for the next shoe to drop. As weird as it sounds, it was true. But I had done the work for years to release that, and I thought I had succeeded. I released theatrics from my life, and peace had found its natural state in our home. I cherished this new peace and thought I had cut drama out like a surgeon cuts out a tumor. But now I was seeing drama again around every curve in the road. Had I really done surgery on this drama thing or had I merely masked it? What was allowing this to come back to me with a vengeance? Was it the house?

I found out from the neighbors that this house was originally owned by a couple who had an elderly parent living with them. They got divorced and sold the house. Maybe it was an impression of that unhappy situation imprinted on the house. Was it Mom being here?

I understood how she thrived on drama. Jean-Pierre had recovered from one bout of pneumonia to find it had come back. He was now on so many pain killers that his brain convinced him his body was in even more pain. Those Lortab pain killers are cunning. I have learned far more than I ever wanted to know about them or ever thought I would. The more I experienced the "system" of taking care of accident victims and their health problems, the more I became jaded by the health care and insurance industry.

Everyone wanted to keep my husband ill and junked up. The system is set up that way, for us to hand over blindly the precious commodity of our physical bodies. I was tireless in my pursuit to help Jean-Pierre, searching holistic doctors, acupuncturists, special diets and supplements.

He would do almost anything I suggested, but I needed to tell him about it at the right time when he was open to it. I became a pro at knowing when the door was open and when not to say anything. At one point, he went on a two-week milk fast that was recommended by a Chinese Acupuncturist. Now that is willpower! It is an amazing trait he has to stick it out. Once he decides to do something, he does it. The milk diet did nothing but probably bring up his cholesterol. There was sometimes temporary relief, but nothing significant. Work was nearly impossible for him at times, as he could not get around with his back, and sometimes he could not focus through the pain. His natural grimace became more pronounced as the muscles in his face showed the world his internal struggle of physical and emotional angst.

Jean-Pierre had become deeply pessimistic and sarcastic. He started every response to a question or statement with a negative and debunked my opinion. His view on anything had a film of cynicism on it. I continued to muster up empathy for him but, as the years went on, I became weary of living with the pessimism. He would never acknowledge it, and we would even argue about whether he was negative or not. I began to understand that this journey for him was his own, and that no one was going to find an answer but Jean-Pierre.

Our marriage was slipping away, and I wondered if he knew it. How could he not? I would mention, discuss, beg, and write emails and letters to him, with every kind of analogy relating to "tending to a garden." "If you don't tend to the garden (our relationship), it will die. It takes two to tango," and so forth, but it never seemed to impact him as warning signs.

I needed help. Serious help. Where to find it? I started to look under trees and bushes. It was time to put my unconscious and unwritten plan into action. I was going to open myself to more non-traditional solutions, and step out into Las Vegas in search of spiritual and healing answers for Jean-Pierre, Mom, and me.

With this new approach I was having glimpses to possible solutions. I read and watched inspiring movies, and with each book, New Age conversation (or, as it is now called, New Thought), and each practice, I found some relief. New Thought is the concept that one Conscious Being unites all, that all is connected, and that we are able to create our reality with infinite possibilities. Some may say, this is not New Thought but rather Ancient Wisdom.

The movie The Secret led me to more understanding of The Law of Attraction. It was subtle, but it was something. I hung on to information from books, DVDs, and psychic readings and explored crystals as talismans and lifelines. Here was hope.

It was like looking for breadcrumbs along the path for answers. One thing led me to another and to another and, with each feeling of some relief or excitement, it led me to the next. During visits to a local Metaphysical shop, I became highly interested in crystals. I found out which ones would be helpful for pain, breaking through depression, for sleep disorders, and many other possibilities for Jean-Pierre.

I bought dozens of penny and nickel-sized smooth tumbled stones in varied colors and intentions: Black Apache Tear and grey Smokey Quartz for blocking negative energies, Black Obsidian for healing and releasing energy blockages, which is meant to help one work quickly to move truths to the surface so that the issue can be resolved, beautiful pink Rose Quartz for unconditional love, and so on. I learned about oracle and affirmation cards and pendulums for divining answers to questions.

I was introduced to chakras, which are the energy centers of our physical and nonphysical bodies, and how stresses block these energy vortexes. I explored each stone I was attracted to and then looked up their properties in the Crystal Bible or Love Is in the Earth crystal books to understand their meaning and usefulness. More breadcrumbs were being placed as clues in my path of expansion, with conversations and synchronicities, and each acknowledgement brought me more relief.

Back home, I placed the crystals under Jean-Pierre's pillow and under the mattress on his side of our bed. As I did this, I felt overcome with compassion for my husband's pain. Maybe these crystals did have supernatural power. I literally prayed they did:

"Dear God, I am at my breaking point. Please shine the light on this situation. Give me a sign. Help these crystals work for us. Give me the answer. Why is there so much trouble in our family? I am exhausted by fighting this uphill battle. I have always been a believer in you and that love will conquer all, but I am not so sure now. I am falling apart. Please help me find the answers."

I waited for a day. Then a week. Then two. Nothing. Maybe a healing miracle was coming, but not through the crystals under Jean-Pierre's pillow. However, there were subtle changes occurring and, although the breakthroughs were not visually significant, a shifting was occurring in each one of us - or was it just me?

Remain faithful to the light .... Remember, the sun is shining behind the clouds

~Wayne Dyer~

I was sick again. The illnesses started coming about every other week. Nothing huge, mind you, just constant - colds, upper respiratory infections, urinary tract infections, and sinus infections.

I made an appointment with our naturopathic physician, Dr. Wright whom friends had recommended some years prior, and we all started to see her. She incorporates bio-energetics with state-of-the-art equipment approved by the FDA which measures body balance through pressure points in your hands and feet.

This is not like any other doctor's office, traditional or holistic, that I have ever experienced. There is a folding table which holds a laptop computer hooked to extension apparatus. The patient holds one of them, a conductor rod, in one hand and Dr. Wright sprays a small amount of water in that hand. Then she uses another probe and pushes firmly on acupuncture points on your feet and hands. With each probe, the computer screen shows whether the indication of that organ or issue is in balance or not.

Then she frowned at me. "What are you doing to yourself, girl?" she asked in a no-nonsense Southern style.

"You are still young and you need to do something about the amount of stress you have, or there will be consequences."

Dr. Wright was right! I was clinging onto my new business for dear life, a marriage that was not fulfilling, and a commitment and obligation to care for my mother who didn't appear to appreciate it. The real estate market was in freefall. It was clear Las Vegas was going to be hit hard. No one was spending money on advertising or magazine profiles that sustained my faltering business. But I had spent so much money, energy, and time on this venture. The weight of obligation I felt to my friend and business partner and investors was staggering.

Again, my mantra was, "I won't give up, even if it kills me."

What happened next is important to my story. I didn't know it yet, but I was about to be given a glimpse into the all-knowing. The look behind the veiled curtain of our world helped lead me to my intended destiny: specifically, healing the trouble in my family and expanding as the being I am meant to be. Watching The Secret, and reading other texts in the field of New Thought, had opened the door to the concept of "synchronicity." This is the idea that there are no coincidences in life, only a world full of guided signs along the path to your destiny.

All you have to do is develop your intuition, recognize and follow the guided signs, and choose and allow your path. Acting on the signs or markers is the key, and almost as important, allowing for it all to unfold without the resistance of uncertainty.

But I was somewhat new at this and extremely tentative. As I attempted to read the signs, I was constantly practicing a kind of clumsy novice's bargaining with the Universe. It makes me laugh at myself now when I look back on it. But I also know that my stumbles and falls might help others starting to practice their own connection to Spirituality.

My bargaining went like this: signs needed to come to me in threes. If I felt I was receiving a sign, I would ask the Universe for a second and then a third as backups to the original. "This could be a coincidence," I would say. Speaking to the unseen Universe of consciousness, I would add, "If you would send me another sign, I could be sure."

A striking instance of this beginner's dilemma awaited me on this very day in the parking lot outside Dr. Wright's office. As I walked to my car worrying about my life dilemmas, I heard a voice speaking in my ear, clearly and in a normal tone, as if the speaker was standing next to me. Only I was completely alone. "Ray-Key" was my phonetic interpretation of what the voice said. I opened the car door, sat down and experienced a deep emotional knowing that something important had just occurred. But the novice in me sat on the fence. "Was that in my head?" I wondered. "Am I going mad?" Or, was that a huge neon flashing sign? For a fleeting moment, I tried to rationalize the experience saying I was tired, maybe I was just hearing the wind…etc.

I knew a bit about Reiki. It's a Japanese spiritual healing practice, some say with roots in Buddhism as the system's founder had a Buddhist orientation. Reiki practitioners believe they pass Universal energy, known as "ki" through their palms, promoting equilibrium and self-healing as they pass their hands on or above the bodies of those receiving the treatment.

I had sampled Reiki 10 years before from my eldest sister, Sophie, but I didn't get anything out of it, or so I thought. Later, my sister Delphine became a Reiki practitioner and has performed "distance Reiki" on me and my mother. When Delphine offered this, I remember thinking it seemed impossible for healing energy to travel coast to coast. But I had to admit, after my treatment I definitely felt rested and calm.

Sitting in my car after hearing the phantom voice, I felt drawn to believe that this was a message from beyond. I wanted to follow the sign, connect the dots between my health problems and Reiki, and seek a Reiki practitioner. But I wobbled. Maybe the voice was imagined. I asked the Universe for another sign so I could be sure. Exactly one day later, my cousin Annie in Los Angeles called me to discuss an article she had just read on ways to relieve stress by detoxing the body and emotions. The author listed Reiki as one of the methods. When I arrived home later in the day, a fax from Annie was waiting. It was the article we spoke about. I can't remember the last time I received a fax that was not a real estate contract. Light bulb: surely this was No. 2 on the sign meter, wasn't it?

I was so struck by this development that I said to myself I didn't even need a third sign. I was excited that I received this second sign so significantly and quickly. I vowed to find a practitioner for a Reiki treatment. But life got in the way, and I did not seek a practitioner.

I didn't know where to find one. I learned that we don't vault into Spirituality in one flawless leap. It takes time, patience, and back-sliding and mistakes to train our intuition to serve us on our spiritual path. After all, we have free-will in play and if we do not actually follow the signs or breadcrumbs, you will stop seeing them.

For me, beginning my spiritual exploration was an exercise in almost random fits and starts more than it was a discipline. Mostly, I took direction from friends. Over long lunches, my lovely and supportive friend Brenda and I compared notes on our spiritual explorations. Brenda had been a spiritual seeker for more than 20 years, and was an avid student of Deepak Chopra and the Chopra Center, as well as Esther and Jerry Hicks, among many other leaders in spiritual consciousness.

Brenda would give me tips on meditation and quieting my mind, such as slowing down the breath and choosing an appropriate time and place. I tried to meditate in the way she advised, but I could not quiet my chattering mind. So I tried to control it instead. Everything had to be perfect for me to attempt a meditation. The room had to be decorated just so, with Buddha or statuary of spiritual masters, the temperature not too cool and not too warm, and I had to have candles, the perfect incense, and a soft seat or cushion. The room had to be lit just so and in silence… absolute silence. If the stars were aligned as well, I might eek out two minutes of meditation. Can anyone say Control Freak?

From my wonderful friend, and later business partner, Paul, I learned about automatic writing. It is said that the Spirit world can take over the writing hand of a person to communicate from the non-physical realm. One might write out a question and then wait in a relaxed, meditative state for the answer to be produced. Paul joked about his early experiences when he was guided to do automatic writing by a close friend and mentor.

He would sit and wait with pencil in hand in quiet meditation. One day he received a phone call from his mentor who advised him, if he wants to actually experience automatic writing, he must open his eyes! Interesting how he "knew" what Paul was doing during his writing sessions alone. I wanted some of that experience, too, so I carved out 30 minutes to sit with pencil in hand, relaxing and waiting for something to happen. But I got bored after 15 minutes. I had produced nothing more than a microscopic pencil scribble in the center of a loose-leaf notebook. So my investigations evolved as a daisy chain from crystals, meditation, and automatic writing to angel cards and lucid dreaming.

I was dabbling, barely scratching the surface of Spirituality or New Thought. But still, I was pushing forward as best I knew how amid daily responsibilities. And this brings me to another lesson about beginning spiritual practice, perhaps the most inspiring lesson of all. If you make a mistake, keep going. Wake up! In a world filled with guided signs, you will get another chance to find your way along your path. That's what was about to happen to me in a most extraordinary way.

It started on the day of my second attempt at automatic writing. Concerned, as usual, about setting a perfect stage, I shut myself in my bedroom and sat at my beloved teak antique desk, the one I had bought 20 years prior in Baltimore on a shopping excursion with my mother. As always, we negotiated the deal beautifully with the resale shop. Now I lit candles and incense and added soft background music to relax me. Mom was out at the hairdresser. Jean-Pierre was working in his home office. Luke was at day care. As a warm-up, I gave myself a predictive reading with angel cards, then picked up my pencil, closed my eyes (even though the advice of Paul's mentor was not to), and waited. I decided to call upon my deceased father for assistance. Something felt different today. My hand started to move. Deep inside me, a feeling of beauty filled my being. My mind started to race with excitement that something was happening. I was getting a communication, but then the pencil stopped. I had produced a larger scribble, but certainly nothing that could be remotely viewed as words. Still, the momentous feeling stayed with me. I was getting somewhere; I didn't want to stop. I decided to meditate.

Putting down the pencil, I started to quiet my mind, still sitting in the chair. My father came to my mind again. So, I asked his Spirit to come and help me meditate and to please give me a message. I began to let go of everything around me, all thought, and just relaxed in the "being" state. It was working.

Then the internal dialogue. "Okay, I am getting there. Stop talking. You are going to mess it up. Just let it happen. Okay, stop thinking. Stop talking. Is something happening?"

Then, I experienced a total release like a switch was turned off; I started to drift.

While I was in this deeply-relaxed state, nothingness in my mind and mind's eye, it was as if I were in a dark hole. Then, toward the upper right side of my internal vision, a light came from the distance. The light moved closer, then turned into a picture, and I saw the Blessed Mother. Clearly. So clearly. Beautiful!

The vision was not her entire body, but rather her head and upper body only. A long scarf gently rested over her head. I immediately burst into a sob that took me to my knees. The emotion welled up so fast, I was taken off guard - from peacefulness to an outburst of emotion in seconds. I realized that I felt unworthy of this visit. She communicated with me without moving her lips.

"The Queen of the Angels" is what I heard in my mind, and the word "compassion."

I was crying so hard I broke the connection to the meditation and to my visitor. This was powerful. I leaned back on my legs as I had dropped to the floor on my knees, and I continued to cry for about 30 minutes. I couldn't stop. I had just witnessed and participated in a full-blown holy visitation from Mary, the Blessed Mother of Jesus Christ, with whom I had no prior connection and, dare to say, belief.

Why would the Blessed Mother come to me in my own bedroom? I wondered. I was scared. I was confused. I felt unworthy. The Blessed Mother? Why me? I am not devoted to her. Still, I believed in her message for me. "Compassion." she had said. I took this to mean I must show Jean-Pierre more compassion as he struggled with his pain, addiction, unhappiness, and growing impatience with him. That must be it. I felt a sense of relief and gratitude for the message.

"I can do that," I thought. "I can be more compassionate."

I found myself in a daze after this experience; a weird sense of disbelief and uneasiness coupled with awe. I had not been getting along well with Jean-Pierre, so I didn't feel like I could share something like this. He would just dismiss it anyway. I also didn't want to share with him that I needed to have more compassion for him, and that this advice had come from a very high source.

I composed myself and told Jean-Pierre, "I need to go out for a bit. I will be picking Mom up from the hairdresser, and I will be home later."

It was Friday, and Mom had a standing appointment at a local salon, so my errand was nothing out of the usual. It wasn't quite time to pick her up when I left the house, so I sat in the car and my mind rested on Jean-Pierre. He was on his spiritual path years before I met him, and he understood the process. But was he still on that path, or had he been kicked off the path since he had lost his business, since we had come together, or since the accident or moving to Vegas?

Before we married, Jean-Pierre had gone into the wilderness for a camping trip alone to commune with the Universe. He will tell you "I made a conscious decision to ask Lee to marry me. I did not take the decision lightly as being on your Spiritual path is a selfish one. Not in a bad way, but it is something you do alone. I decided to help Lee on her path, and I asked her to marry me."

Where was Jean-Pierre on his path now? I wondered. Had he helped me on mine and if so, in what ways? Was his job done? I dialed Mom's cell phone.

"Hi Mom, we are going to go have lunch. Okay?"

"Hot Dogs!" she replied in her excitement that we would not be going straight home.

"No, not hot dogs Mom, but a real lunch." We both laughed. She loves hot dogs. Not knowing why, I now felt compelled to blurt out, "I need to go to the Ross – Dress for Less store. Can we go there first before lunch?"

"Sure," Mom replied. "What do you need to get?"

"Nothing. I just feel like I need to go there."

Mom agreed. She loved to shop, and we could always pass time browsing anywhere.

Parked in a prime spot in the parking lot next to Ross, I began to share with Mom my experience, as she is open to any kind of news. She is a great listener.

She listened just as she would to any tale I might share from an ordinary day, but I was not certain she was grasping the enormity of this one. I wrapped up the story by saying,

"I guess it is compassion that I need more of with the situation with Jean-Pierre. So what do you think?"

There was a bit of delay before she began to talk. I thought maybe she hadn't been listening and got startled by my question.

"Well," Mom replied in a somewhat disheartened manner with even a twinge of annoyance, "Why did the Blessed Mother come to YOU when I am the one who has been devoted to her all these years?"

I was a bit taken by surprise at her personal affront in making this story about herself. Then I realized "I am such an idiot." The message that came from Mother Mary was not about Jean-Pierre - it was Mom who needed my compassion. Of course!

Initially, my reaction to Mom's comment was that of judgment at her bringing the story around to herself. Then, just as quickly, I recognized why she was expressing a jealousy of the message. It was brilliant contrast and even more a perfect sign.

Wasn't this a perfectly normal reaction from someone who was so devoted to the Blessed Mother for the past 80-some years? "I don't know, Mom," I said. "Let's go inside."

At that moment, something – I did not know what – was pulling on me like a magnet. I was a woman on a mission, striding through the double glass doors with Mom following behind me, as if I knew where I was going. I was still pondering what had occurred with my conversation with Mom in the car and still feeling the aftermath of my visitation. I headed straight back to the far end of the store where the housewares were displayed. At the back wall, I stopped in my tracks. It was as though I were seeing a ghost. There was a wall full of twenty or so framed pictures depicting the Blessed Mother. "Oh my God, Mom, do you see this?" I asked.

"Oh, those are lovely," she replied lightly, as if I had never even told her my story.

"So, you really did come to me, didn't you?" I said out loud to the Blessed Mother pictures. For some time, I couldn't stop looking into the holy faces that had altered my life. The Blessed Mother DID come for Mom, just via me.

As of this moment, two weeks had now passed since my medical appointment with Dr. Wright, but considering everything that had happened, it seemed like two lifetimes. Now I was back in her office for a follow-up visit. As I stood writing my check on the small ledge at the reception window, I accidentally knocked over a small business card holder. The cards fell to the floor.

Embarrassed by my clumsiness, I reached down for the cards and discovered they had all fallen, shiny side up, displaying the words "Reiki Master."

Light bulb, ding, ding; it was the third message, the one I hadn't even asked for but needed to get me going again... Maria Queen, the Reiki Master, was right here in Dr. Wright's office. She had been here the whole time. All I needed to do was call her. I telephoned that very same day and made an appointment.

My Spirit was awakening. I was no longer the fumbling novice who lacked conviction to read the signs. I had connected with the Blessed Mother in meditation. I had found my way to Reiki.

CHAPTER 6   ARE YA FLOATIN YET?

Life has no limitations, except the ones you make
~Les Brown~

She was not what I anticipated. On the phone Maria sounded less gentle than my imaginary Reiki Master would be, with a smoker's gravelly voice. I had envisioned a gentle, motherly-type person who spoke softly in a melodic tone, and who was patient and loving. After getting over the initial surprise and hesitation, I asked Maria Queen questions that she seemed impatient to answer. However, I wasn't going to miss this sign. I made an appointment for the next day.

Maria's small treatment room had a massage table in the center, shelves and tables filled with crystals, a heater for hot stones, books, a small desk area with computer, and peaceful mood music playing. The walls were adorned with inspirational pictures, art, and quotations. I already had an affinity for crystals and stones by this time. I was even picking up everyday rocks and pine cones along walks with some regularity and weird attraction. The pine cone affinity I have had since I was a child though.

The soft sound of water running through the fountain and the palpable feeling of higher energy in Maria's room ushered me off to my Reiki experience. Maria took time to explain that Reiki was the Universal Life Force Energy that we all have access to.

"You lie on the table fully clothed, except for removing your shoes and jewelry," she said, as I had already started to take off my shoes while sitting on the side chair. She continued her explanation as I removed my necklace and watch; I situated myself on the massage table face up.

"When a Reiki practitioner is attuned into Reiki, it is done through a ceremony overseen by a Reiki Master," Maria explained. "The process opens the person's higher chakras to allow for the Life Force Energy to flow through them and out of their hands to the one in need of healing."

The concept of chakras dates from ancient Hindu teachings, describing a series of circular energy fields in the human body from the base root chakra at the bottom of the spine to the crown chakra just above the top of the head. Chakras are believed to be the focal points through which the human body sends and receives energy.

"The practitioner is a vessel," Maria explained. "I can't control it. The energy will flow where it needs to for the healing."

She started by placing her warm hands on my head, and I felt them get noticeably hotter. Then Maria began to work down my body, quietly she worked placing her hands on specific areas. As she methodically moved her hands down to my neck and heart area, belly, and legs, I was feeling an incredible sense of peace and well-being. I felt an enormous amount of heat coming from Maria's hands. I didn't know what she was doing, but I felt wonderful. I was relaxing and letting go.

This was especially amazing in a new environment where I had no idea what to expect; this was quite a feat. During the session, I fell into a blissful state of being present but not asleep. Thoughts would come to me, and then I would acknowledge them, and send them on their way easily, as if I had done this many times before. I really needed this sense of peace. My body and Spirit were tired.

Just then, I started to lift. When I say "I," I mean the "I" that is not my physical body, but rather the essence of me. My Spirit started to lift outside my body, although I was totally conscious, extremely relaxed, but aware. I remember the sensation so clearly that, as it started to happen, I got scared and consciously pulled myself back. But the sensation was too amazing and too good to give up entirely. I allowed it to happen again, and even to extend a little further out. I allowed my "I" to go, and then I pulled myself back again as an exercise to know that I was controlling it. It was such an easy-flowing sensation of fluid light and peace. Although I was gently lifting outside my body, I was not above my body or able to see my physical self.

On the third release of "I" out of my body, I heard Maria ask, "Are ya floatin' yet?" in her gravelly voice.

I could barely contain myself. I pulled myself back in and asked: "You can see me?" I was so naïve to the process of energy work that I actually thought she might be looking at my Spirit floating outside my body. Maria laughed in her rough way, and said that she could feel my energy lifting. That was so cool. The ride continued.

Subsequently, I have come to understand that this energy Maria was channeling does not discriminate. I used to believe that you needed to be specially gifted to access psychic abilities, speak to dead relatives, or to channel energy healing. No longer. It is available to anyone and everyone. We all have access.

When the session was over, Maria explained that I should drink a lot of water and rest, if possible, for the remainder of the day. "When is that going to happen?" I thought. Luckily, it was already late afternoon, and I talked myself into chilling without guilt. I felt so amazing that I really could not have concentrated on work anyway. The floating Spirit experience was so profound that I called my mother, my cousin, and Delphine on the ride home to tell them about it. I felt wiped out; my body felt like it had been run over by a truck. The most extraordinary part was that my Spirit still felt dislodged from my physical body. I was in an altered state.

I knew this was a breakthrough. The question was how to extend the relaxation of Reiki into my chaotic life. I got the opportunity soon enough. "We need a break," Jean-Pierre announced out of the blue one day. He was starting to find his way out of the rabbit hole he had been living in, and now proposed the idea that we take a family holiday to visit his parents in France.

We had not taken any vacation in so long and, if we could swing it, it would be a well-deserved rest. How would we do that financially? Jean-Pierre had closed on some real estate deals and all we needed to do was get the airfare, and some spending money. His parents would take care of the rest as we would be staying with them.

Jean-Pierre realized we had air miles on American Express that would conveniently take us to Nice, near where his parents lived. Luke was three years old, and Jean-Pierre's parents had not seen him since he was an infant. It was time for a trip to the South of France.

My initial reaction to the idea of this trip was not one you might expect from a sane person. I was not excited or exhilarated. I was panic-stricken, as I thought about leaving my business on life support after the latest gut-wrenching setback: the sudden death of an angel investor who had promised infusion of capital that was supposed to give us one last chance to survive. "I can't go!" I said. "There is no way I can go! You and Luke will have to go without me! How can I leave Mom and the business?" It was the old me, the pre-Reiki me, speaking, and I flinched to hear myself using the negative tone of "No, I can't."

Being the dutiful and supportive husband that Jean-Pierre was, he simply said, "Okay, Luke and I will go."

But it wasn't so simple. As I sat in my home office that was a revamped dining room diligently working on my monthly column for the e-zine, I pursued a lively internal conversation.

"What, are you crazy? What person in their right mind says no to an opportunity like this? You are tired. You need a break. Mom can go back East for a visit. It would be good for her to get away from the intense summer heat here. You need to go. Jean-Pierre and I need this alone time to rekindle our relationship. We need some fun."

That was the new me talking, making a decision that would set the stage for another unraveling of life as I knew it.

Even before we left, I had a feeling that I needed to go on this trip as part of an invisible plan. Deep down in every part of my being I knew that when I returned, my life would never be the same. I did not know why or how but just that it was so. It scared me deeply. But that trip to Cannes was one of the most beautiful I have ever experienced, and I have previously been fairly well-traveled for an American. It was exactly what the doctor ordered for this small family on life support.

I felt so grateful and appreciative for the opportunity, and I cherished every moment. I rested.

The break from living with my mother was much needed for our marriage as well. It had been four years since we moved Mom cross-country to live with us, and the scars of the reality of that decision and Jean-Pierre's accident were showing.

Jean-Pierre too, needed some reflective time. He was still working through the depths of his own personal journey after the accident. The trip also gave him and me the opportunity to reconnect, as our personal intimate relationship was severely suffering with the lack of privacy. Too many important things were just left unsaid and unfelt.

The sea air, the daily playful pool time with Luke, the late morning walks down to the local marketplace, the nurturing energy of family, and the healing sun were the perfect medicine.

The French know how to live. Everything is a slower pace, except maybe the passionate way they argue and enjoy sport. They walk to the market and they spend time cooking, and they certainly spend time eating and conversing. Jean-Pierre and I started to feel intimate sparks again, as we would steal time during siesta to make love after a beautiful lunch prepared by his mother that included a gorgeous French Rosé wine. With Luke down for a nap; the shuttered windows opened on the second floor, with the sea breeze and the air smelling ever so sweet, we reunited.

We explored each other's bodies for the first time in so long and that seemed to reawaken our desire for each other. It was long overdue. We were playful again, cuddled, and remembered we loved each other.

Our time away went by in a blink. Mid-August, we started traveling back from Nice by way of New York and through customs. This occurred during a time where there were terrorist activities and heighted airport security. Traveling was certainly less interesting than it used to be. I kept a close eye and hand on Luke, as Jean-Pierre managed the process of customs and luggage. Jean-Pierre received our bags in New York and checked them back in headed for Las Vegas. We got settled in for the last leg of the trip. So far so good.

It was pretty much an uneventful trip traveling home, although long and exhausting with a toddler. Arriving in Las Vegas had another tale to tell. When we went to baggage claim, all the luggage arrived except mine.

My two bags never made it to the Las Vegas baggage claim. Airline representatives assured me that they would find them. Due to the increased security, especially at international airports, I had pared down my carry-on to only what was necessary for Luke. He was still very young, and his needs were very particular for what pacified him for such a long trip. This meant that things that I would normally carry on with me, such as important items or valuables, would need to be packed in checked luggage.

I supported the power of positive thought and was getting comfortable with the idea of healing energy, so I envisioned white light around my luggage to keep it safe on the journey. So I packed my keepsakes and valuable jewelry in my suitcase that August day.

My in-laws are "old school" in the fact that they very much respect the dining and presentation experience, and the way that one dresses for such an outing. I honor this with them and appreciate their ways, so when I packed, I packed my finest things including: a diamond necklace; a platinum, diamond, topaz, and onyx ring I had purchased in Italy on a vacation some years prior, that I had only worn on special occasions; sentimental gifts from my husband, my mother, and friends; special pieces of jewelry that had been bought over the years; and beautiful handmade, one-of-a-kind pieces specifically purchased from a dear friend and designer. In addition, I had recently bought a new wardrobe after losing significant baby weight.

Before the trip, I painstakingly bargain shopped for these new clothes because of our limited funds. Then in France, Jean-Pierre's parents watched Luke for a couple of days while we met London friends in Paris. There I splurged on some stunning jewel-colored cashmere sweaters and lovely pieces of Parisian clothing that had been heavily reduced from the previous year and would be perfect for the fall. All gone! Books, belts, accessories, mementos, perfume we bought in France, my prescription glasses, and so on. All vanished! I visited the police, I detailed the loss, I dug up receipts and pictures, I wrote reports, and spent hours at the airport police department only to be told that it was taken in Las Vegas and that they would handle it.

One might think that the process of dealing with the police, the paperwork, and the insurance company would help in some small way to give a sense of constructive assistance and defuse the emotion from all of this. But it only deepened my sense of loss. Each hour and day that passed, I would recall something else that was missing and have this deep feeling of violation and loss.

Bits and pieces of my life, as expressed through purchases and gifts, took on such emotional weight. I cried and mourned my things for weeks as I retold the story to anyone who would listen. The empathy that I received from others only made me feel worse. "You poor thing," friends would say. This time, that old haunting phrase was true. Yes, I was a poor thing. I grieved my things more significantly than I wanted to openly admit. And, on top of it, the insurance company was only covering a fraction of the monetary loss.

The next hit was that we had unexpected bills arise that stifled my ability to repurchase anything because we needed to pay bills with the reimbursement money. I wasn't finding a silver lining anywhere. "I know there is a lesson in all of this!" I exclaimed through sobbing eyes to my friend Wendy over the phone on week two of the saga. Then it dawned on me like a ton of bricks! My tears started to dry up as I exclaimed, "Oh my God, I am an idiot!" Clarity struck. "The lesson is Attachment!!"

The message is that I was too attached to my stuff, that things can't bring happiness. Could it be that simple?

Meanwhile, Wendy quietly allowed me space to express this stream of consciousness.

"Certainly every single person that I told this story to would have gotten that message. Why did it take me two weeks? I guess I needed to feel the depth of the loss; I needed it to come full circle."

Wendy simply replied with a "Yes, Honey." In that moment my tears turned to laughter. I felt incredible. Sweet release.

These days, I really was finally getting the message – or, more accurately, the messages, plural. Not just this one about the negative force of material attachments, but other messages from Source. I have come to call God by many names: Source was one of them, Creator, Universe, Divine, and others as I felt compelled. One of the most stunning messages was delivered by Maria, the Reiki Master, in her treatment room where my out-of-body voyages under the influence of Reiki energy were continuing to unfold.

At one Reiki session, Maria revealed that she sometimes received intuitive messages for her clients. She explained that Reiki practitioners must open their crown chakras in order to access the healing energy. This opens the practitioner to receive information from the Spirit world, as well as healing energy. Maria asked if I wanted the messages.

"Heck yeah, I do," I said. "It's like a gift with purchase."

"You are a Light Worker," Maria said, using a baffling term that I didn't really know what it meant. I was totally confused, and didn't know how to make sense of this. On one level, it struck me as some kind of mistake: this simply wasn't me. And yet, as Maria spoke, I was feeling an emotional connection to the word. I thought of the extraordinary morning I woke up and had chosen the name that means Bringer of Light for my unborn child. I thought of the light surrounding the Blessed Mother in my vision of her.

Maria continued, "A Light Worker is someone who works with the energy of the Light to help people on their spiritual path. You will be working in healing and work with writers of spiritual books." If Maria was right, she was foretelling a future for me that would be so dramatically different from my present that it truly sounded like someone else's life.

As far as I knew, I was most definitely the "Light Receiver" and certainly not the Light Worker. But, as events would soon reveal, the truth really is stranger than fiction. A series of incredible twists and turns began the unfolding of the exact destiny Maria was now describing to her incredulous and even doubting client.

CHAPTER 7   THE LIGHT

Awakening into love is a lifelong path

~David Simon~

I love how the Universe works. It is like a "Universal Chess Game," moving people around like chess pieces to connect one to another and allow for the perfect sequence of events to play out their destiny. Jean-Pierre and I are the kind of couple who, even when we are apart for work, are regularly calling and texting each other the news of the day or just to say hello. Since our child was born, the tapestry of our connection has woven even tighter; even through the darkest of time, there is a thread that links us. So for Jean-Pierre to decide to go away on his own, as he did in the summer of 2008, for 10 days with no contact at all, wasn't just unusual, it was not likely. This was the Universe at work, setting the stage for a life-altering awakening.

Jean-Pierre was working on himself to move past the darkness that was initiated, I thought, by his accident and cloaked him like a victim coat. He was already an active spiritual seeker and philosopher when I had met him many years ago. He had trekked Everest; he had lived with Shamans in a tropical rain forest; He took extensive workshops and practiced Vipassana meditation, with extended noble silence.

Although he had not done this type of retreat for many years, actually not since meeting me, he felt an acute urging to go on retreat now as a way to get past the blockage of the accident. Ten days away in silence sounds very difficult, but I supported him 1,000 percent. Even though this trip was on the heels of our return from France, it all just worked out that way with the availability of the retreat. There is no expense to go but gasoline; it was based on service.

Curiously, after a period of improving health, I got sick as he prepared for his trip. A horrific cold had advanced into an upper respiratory infection, my worst one in years. I treated myself with holistic methods, as I had been moving more and more away from traditional medicinal offerings, but they weren't working this time.

Jean-Pierre was apprehensive about leaving Las Vegas as I was so ill, so I scheduled an appointment with our general practitioner doctor who would prescribe antibiotics. On Monday, August 25th, 2008, with much anticipation, Jean-Pierre left Las Vegas for Colorado.

Before he arrived at the retreat and would have to turn off his phone for 10 days, Jean-Pierre called me to chat for the last time. I was just leaving the doctor's office with my prescription to be picked up from the pharmacy. I should have rested, but I didn't. For the next couple of days, I continued with my schedule as usual. I had a sense of urgency to straighten, clean, and pretty-up the house, especially the back patio area.

It was weird - this overwhelming push to put the house in order all of a sudden. What was I preparing for? I even put in an alarm system! I was not sleeping at night, very quickly falling into the depths of illness.

By Thursday, after a couple of days on the antibiotics, there was still no change. Actually, I was feeling much more ill. I called my doctor to tell him that I was getting worse, and he called in another prescription. By Friday, I was on my back. Jean-Pierre had been gone with no contact for about a week. Although I had no fever, I was feeling incredibly unwell.

Saturday came and went without me eating or drinking. "Where is Mom?" I wondered in a dreamlike state. "I need you, Mom." But the words were not reaching my lips. She was nowhere in sight. This was most ironic. One of the challenges of having someone living with you is that they are always there. Always there. I did not even have the strength to call for her. I was barely keeping up with where Luke was, what he was doing, and taking care of his basic needs. I was getting scared.

On Sunday, September 6th, I found myself really fearful. I could now not take care of Luke, and I had no idea what he was up to. I was lying in bed and I could not move my body or lift my head. I mustered enough strength to call my oldest friend Diane, and she offered to keep Luke for the day and overnight. When they left, I crawled back in bed and was immediately spent with exhaustion. I was in and out of consciousness. I couldn't lift my head even to take a drink of water. When was the last time I had any water?

As I rested in the sunlight, I had an incredible sensation that I could die in this moment if I wanted to. Something extraordinary was happening to me. I felt my Spirit lift slightly from my body, similar to the way it did when I had received Reiki for the first time. But this time, I was not able to control it.

I thought, "This is easy. So easy to just let go. It is so peaceful here. Just let go." My thoughts went to Luke.

"If I let myself leave this life, no one would know how to reach Jean-Pierre, and Luke would be alone. He is too young. Mom would be frantic." I was in a twilight stage of consciousness where I could hear the outside world, but I liked where I was in my internal world. I could hear my thoughts, but there was no imagery.

Just then, I went to the most amazing place imaginable: into the Light. I felt instantly calm and peaceful. It was not a place really, but a non-place brilliant with this amazing white light. Whiter than white. Lightening-strike white. The feeling was pure peace and bliss. Sweet. The whiteness was everywhere, and everything, and nothing, all at the same time. It was pure light energy and so was I. It was beautiful, and I had never felt so peaceful and calm and happy in all my life.

I realized I was an energy sphere of light within the context of varying degrees of light, as there was only the contrast to the outer light and the light that was me. I was encased in the most spectacular light, yet, I could still detect the distinction between the light that was all around me and me. I noticed two additional light sources. I knew instinctively that these were Light Beings coming to greet and guide me.

They could take on the faded, illuminated outline of a human being, but mostly they stayed in sphere form. They appeared as larger spheres of light than I was and, in my subconscious mind, I perceived they were in front and slightly above me. Although there were no physical attributes to attach to them, I could perceive a few distinctive characteristics. They had authority and spoke with conviction. They were gentle guides who transmitted very little communication, just what was essential. The Light

Being on the left felt like a male energy and was a bit larger in size or energy field. The female energy was on the right.

They were calm, kind, and loving in their tone and, when they communicated with me, it was a telepathic communication. They were not beings who seemed familiar, such as the spirits of past loved ones or guides that I might have had a hint of in a dream. This was our first meeting. I perceived that this was their job. They had been chosen as my transition guides for a specific expertise that they had...I felt elated, excited, and relieved all at the same time. Woohoo!

My experience of arriving at this unknown destination was something like getting off a roller coaster ride that I had waited for hours to get on. As I was rounding the last freefall, I threw my arms up over my head and yelled with a full belly relief of excitement, "Excellent ride!" That's how I felt in this moment, as the imaginary car was slowing down and coming into the returning platform. I found relief that the ride was over. The rush was great, but it was a challenge on my system. I wanted to go back home... not to Las Vegas, but to the Source of all energy in the Universe - to the Other Side. To death ... to life.

"Not so fast," was the telepathic message my guides now communicated, "Let's review a few things." I eagerly obliged. They held the key to the light train home, interestingly; I didn't have any panic about not having a body. It all seemed natural. It was as if I had done this before. I did feel a bit annoyed about the red tape that I needed to go through, but I would tolerate it so that I could get going. My personality still seemed to be a part of me. That felt unusual. Here I was in this ethereal place in a different dimension of being, but still suffering with my third-dimensional personality flaws, or are they not flaws at all?

My guides and I reviewed my personal relationships. We were going through this intuitive extrasensory list. Oh, wow, I felt such excitement and respect for this soul called Jean-Pierre. It was beautiful. It wasn't about the physical person at all, but rather the energy that he is. The most spectacular feeling of love was permeating through me as I was experiencing my feelings for the soul called Jean-Pierre.

The love was every part of my essence and was enormous in capacity. The love was so potent and overpowering, it was beyond imagination. I realized that my experience of love in my third-dimensional life prior to this was a minuscule speck on the love meter. This was amazing! So much love, so much respect, so much knowledge and wisdom, and absolutely no feeling of attachment.

My vocabulary was ill-equipped to describe this feeling, although I kept grasping for a word or phrase that might fit. But while the experience was happening, no words were needed, just feeling and telepathic communication of that feeling. There was no sense of outcome of a situation relating to Jean-Pierre. No attachment or control, no feeling of loss. Not even a twinge of what his future would be without me. Nothing but pure appreciation of the experience with him and the most amazing feeling of love.

Once the fullness of the internal experience of Jean-Pierre was diminishing and then complete, my guides and I moved to all the key people in my soul group, which I automatically knew was like a team member on earth. Lastly,

I was presented with my son. I felt there to be a strategy going on - for dramatic impact, I suspected.

The immense, overwhelming love and appreciation I had for Luke was such an honor. It was powerful, yet softer than with Jean-Pierre. It held a strong vibration - extreme and intense, but different.

My feeling was that this amazing soul, Luke, had provided me with such knowledge and expansion. It was such a delicious understanding. I felt intense privilege to have optioned the experience of birthing such a beautiful child and mothering him for the last three years. Such gratitude I was feeling. But again, an intense love, but a softer love, and again no attachment prevailed.

As the feeling subsided into the aftermath of deep appreciation and contentment, I began to shift to the trip ahead. "Okay. Let's go!" was my immediate reaction now that I was finished with this part of the debriefing about my life on earth. But again, my guides diverted my excitement for finishing my journey.

"Not so fast," they cautioned, signaling one final delay. We had reached the point of no return. The Light Beings now informed me that the decision was purely mine to make, whether I stayed in my life, or went back to Source. If I so wished, I would be finished with my physical life here and now.

"Great!" I expressed. I wanted to go. But they wanted to be sure I was fully aware of the consequences of my choice.

"It is our responsibility, purpose to provide you with all the information you need for this decision. The most pressing and important one is the child named Luke," my guides solemnly told me. "He is only three years old, and the loss of a mother on the soul of such a young one would have painful residual effects."

I wasn't buying this 100 percent. I even began to plead my case that this young spirit was not young at all, but rather a very old soul, and he was quite independent and a tough little person.

"He is very close to his father, and Jean-Pierre is a good dad, and they would be fine without me," I said. This was certainly not the Lee in the third dimension who was emotionally attached to the love of her son and husband.

The Light Beings seemed to have a job to do: convince me to stay in this world. I perceived they were frustrated by my unwavering desire to leave. They reiterated: "We want you to understand the depth of the loss by experiencing the feeling that the soul Luke would feel at the loss of his mother."

With this consciousness, a feeling of loss; a despair deeper than anything I could imagine rushed through my being like shards of glass tearing through the essence of my soul, more painful than any physical injury inflicted on earth. The depths of this sorrow I would not wish on anyone, much less your child. It changed my decision in an instant.

Promptly, I felt a sense of accomplishment beaming from my guides. They had handled their assignment well. But now I had a final bargain to strike with these eloquent representatives from Source. "Okay, I will go back." I agreed. "I will be Luke's mother, and I will take on the mission of the Light. However, - and I enunciated with a tone of a stern conviction - when my mission is finished and Luke is well on his own path, then I want to return home when I want to return home."

"Agreed." my Light Friends happily acknowledged.

My negotiation continued, "Oh, and I get to do this with no long drawn-out illness or health battle. Deal?" We were done.

"Deal." my guides transmitted to my consciousness as the snow-white scene drifted into darkness.

CHAPTER 8   LIFE AFTER LIGHT

My religion is very simple. My religion is kindness
~The Dalai Lama~

I opened my eyes, and the first thought that came to me was, "What the hell just happened?" The experience could not have lasted more than an hour, or maybe even minutes, as the time was not imprinted on my consciousness nor had I been watching the clock prior, but it was more like the absence of time. In a stupor, I sat up in my bed. "How am I sitting up?" I wondered. It was all feeling very weird.

The room and everything in it was different, somehow more pronounced and radiant. I was trying to digest and understand this new feeling that had washed over me permeating my very being. I had no words.

My Spirit and my body felt as if there was an unexplainable residue of something left on me - indescribable. I had no idea how much time had passed, as I looked around the room and inspected each article in my sight path with wonder and appreciation.

It was as if everything was more alive than before. Even inanimate objects appeared to have a special noticeable beauty. I stared at the door with all its related parts with such pleasure that I knew I needed help to understand what was going on. I couldn't move away from this feeling. I didn't want to. I called my sister, Delphine, on the East Coast – the one who talks to dead people – to gain some insight.

"De, it's Lee. Do you have a minute to talk?" I took a deep breath and began my narrative. "I just had something weird happen to me that feels like … a fantasy of death. There is no other way I can explain it."

"Uh huh," Delphine replied, allowing me to proceed. The words tumbled out so fast I was amazed I was even making sense.

I detailed the entire experience in the Light for Delphine, and she barely expressed a word.

"I opened my eyes and I was back," I told De.

"I was in bed, and I was completely aware of what had just happened. Freaked out, no comprehension, but aware. Not understanding it, except that this was profound. As I slowly awakened more fully, there was a sense of bewilderment. Yet, I was feeling physically significantly better. How can that be? I was feeling like I was on my death bed just moments before. I couldn't lift my head or speak, and now I am sitting up and quite awake, aware, and able to communicate?" I slowed down, took a breath, and asked, "What do you think?"

An outburst of excitement that I did not expect came flooding from the phone.

"You had an exit opportunity!" my sister exclaimed.

"A what?" I asked.

"An exit opportunity!" she repeated. "We all have them apparently; several, in fact in a lifetime, is what I read from Sylvia Browne's book."

"Kind of a get-out-of-jail-free card?" I asked.

Now Delphine was the one talking fast. "Yes, right. Most of the time we do not remember them, but apparently you are supposed to remember it."

There was just a bit too much exuberance here for me to handle just after this journey through space and time. I begged off to get some rest.

I needed more advice; I called my dear friend and spiritual confidant, Brenda. She immediately referred me to her spiritual advisor, Rosa Glenn Reilly, who owned a spiritual center in Houston.

"You had a near death experience," Rosa said matter-of-factly. "I have had three, and this is textbook."

I felt relieved to learn that this could be a normal experience. Rosa explained that this "residue" that I was feeling was truly an imprint of energy from the other side, but that it would slowly dissipate in approximately two weeks. She encouraged me to journal, as this feeling would leave me in time.

It was amazing how much better I felt. My mood was full of bliss and contentment. I was able to receive Luke back to the house, and we ate and played as I was quickly regaining my strength, still all the while experiencing the enormous reward of this residue of appreciation and awareness all around me. I always love being with Luke, but now there was an added knowledge and deepening of being present with him that was pure joy - purer love than I had ever known. I held him close as he fell asleep, and my gratitude to the Light Beings for steering me back for this spectacular child will forever be etched in my heart.

Monday morning came with peace and joy. I was still deeply contemplating the experience. Brighter walls, livelier sunrise, purer morning! I had touched Spirit, the Creator, the Divine, and God. All those names do not fully classify the One, but rather they are the One. They and others are all names for the one Source. I know for sure now. My mind was analyzing the context surrounding the last day and connecting the dots of the experience - mind, body, and soul. What led to this and what was to come?

My thoughts continued to process my experience: We are all related in this amazing threading of an energetic grid that is the One. We are the One kept ringing back so plainly. "One" and "Light" were continuing to ring back and forth in my consciousness, and then my memories took me back to how we came to naming Luke, the Bringer of Light. Now I knew that moment was prophecy.

I was ready to settle back into normal life, but what is normal now? While brushing my teeth, I felt a strange sensation as I was moving the toothbrush along my teeth and gums. I could not hold my lips closed. "Huh, that is strange," I thought. It was still dark in the bathroom, so I could not properly see in the mirror. I did not want to wake Luke, who was sleeping with me, by turning on the switch, because the sun was not yet beaming through the window. So, I navigated quietly and stepped into the shower while he slept in the master bedroom. Nothing unusual until I tilted my head up toward the shower head and realized I couldn't close my mouth. My heart jumped, and I gazed into the magnifying mirror in the shower. From the morning light that was just beginning to stream in from the window, I could see that the right side of my face was drooping. I looked like I was straight from a horror zombie movie. My eye and mouth were paralyzed.

The sensation of shock fell away within seconds, which was certainly unlike me. I felt no fear. I started laughing. I had this feeling well up in me that was incredible. I felt connected to the Universe. With some exuberance, I pointed to the ceiling with an accusatory finger and shouted, "That is enough! I got the message! No more. I will start the process!" And I carried on getting ready for my day, getting Luke off to school, chatting with my mother like nothing had happened.

This was a new me. I was not fearful. The drama that could be manifested with this situation was not there. I had no attachment to my physical appearance, no feeling of "what is happening to me?" It was such an odd sensation not having the use of half my face, and not being able to close my right eye, but instead of fear or any negative feeling, I felt amused. I was calm. I felt clarity. After dropping Luke off at his preschool, I immediately went to the emergency room at St. Rose Hospital just 5 minutes away. Even walking into the hospital, I had no anxiety. I knew this was a message from my Spirit guides on the other side. I contemplated that my friends, the Light Beings, wanted to give me an outward reality to remember my experience.

I walked up to the desk and pointed, circling with my finger around my face in a sort of playful way "Can you do something about this?" A nurse hurried me into the back examination area as if my situation was critical. I did not feel this at all. I knew that my Spirit friends were just sending me a message.

I figured I had two choices, a stroke or Bell's Palsy. A doctor arrived some moments later and quickly diagnosed me with Bell's Palsy, a form of facial paralysis resulting from a dysfunction of the facial nerve which results in the inability to control facial muscles on the affected side. Several conditions can cause facial paralysis, e.g., brain tumor, stroke, virus, and Lyme disease. However, if no specific cause can be identified, the condition is known as Bell's Palsy and is often mistakenly used as a generic, catch-all term to describe facial paralysis. I would like to add another to the list of causes...Spirit reminders.

The emergency room doctor said it was a good thing that I had come in immediately, as the anti-viral and steroids that they will give me work best upon initial onset.

"You may or may not get the full use of your facial muscles back," he said. "There is a good chance with the medicine being taken at onset that you will fully recover within 6 months to a year."

He gave me the prescription and sent me on my way. While waiting to check out, I had an internal conversation.

"This is a wakeup call. Somebody is trying to tell me to be more present and slow down. My life is not about material things or possessions or anything physical."

There was an interesting calm that I experienced. No drama felt. No stress. I was constantly astonished by the lack of fear and drama during this time. I was grateful for the experience, even for the condition of facial paralysis. I wanted to know what it all meant. I knew I needed to recreate my life. I said a prayer: "Help me to enjoy the simple, beautiful things every day as I see them now, and find a deeper meaning to the day-to-day life I am living."

More than ever, I needed to be true to myself and my guidance, to not make decisions based on fear, obligation or guilt.

Connecting to the Light of Oneness with love in my heart and faith that I am cared for, watched over, and guided always gives me peace.

From the car, I called my working business partner in the online magazine endeavor, Rebecca.

"Rebecca, it is time to let go. Our business is sucking the life from us." We decided by year's end we would close the publishing company. Ahh, relief!

Later I learned by reading Louise Hay's book, You Can Heal Your Life, that Bell's Palsy is related to "extreme control over anger and an unwillingness to express feelings."

Was I angry? Yes, I suppose so. I was angry that Jean-Pierre had been in the car accident that changed everything about what I thought our lives would be, angry that the promise of our lives together did not turn out to be what we had planned, angry that my mother was not who I thought she was, and angry that I could not make the new business work.

Wow, it all came flooding in and out. Later that Monday, I called my acupuncturist and Maria, the Reiki Master, scheduling appointments. With their help and prescription medicine, I regained nearly full feeling in my face in six weeks, except for a right eye that remains more open than the left and is more noticeable when I am tired. It gives me a reminder. I am appreciative of it.

The next day was Tuesday, September 9th. Jean-Pierre was to be coming out of his retreat, and it was Luke's fourth birthday! It was approximately 6 a.m., when Jean-Pierre called.

The first thing that came from his mouth was, "Is everything okay? I have just felt like something was seriously wrong there. I could not meditate at all."

Jean-Pierre drove straight through, which took him 2 days on the outbound trip, to get home to us. He was in an extremely aware and thoughtful space while listening to my experience step-by-step. He hardly said a word. I had to keep reminding myself that he had been in quiet contemplation for 10 days. I knew it was not uncommon for those returning from noble silence to be less than talkative. But then it hit me, and I just blurted out my realization:

"You don't believe me."

"This is weird," I thought, because the feeling for me was that it didn't matter. I did not experience the learned response of rejection, hurt, abandonment, or anything related to self-worth. I was free. Jean-Pierre replied in a very precise and thought-out way, as only Jean-Pierre does.

"No ..." (pause) "I believe you believe that you had an experience," he said. "The mind is a very complex and incredible machine that can trick you into believing."

At that moment, I had this overwhelming feeling of expansion, like the Grinch from the childhood Christmas classic, The Grinch Who Stole Christmas, at the top of Mt. Crumpet when his heart grew three sizes.

"Jean-Pierre,...(pause) it really doesn't matter that you don't believe me. This was the most profound experience of my life, and only I know what I experienced, and what I have felt since touching the Other Side. It has changed me."

To have this experience and not feel the judgment of Jean-Pierre not believing me or the judgment of myself not caring that he did not believe me, was awesome. I loved him every bit as much as I did before, but I felt no attachment toward him. I didn't need him to make me feel any particular way or to fill me up in any way.

Still, walking in these new shoes was going to take some getting used to. Up was down. Messages were in. Real estate was out. I had promised beings from beyond a veil to undertake a "Mission of Light." And, if Maria, the psychic Reiki Master, was on target, I was supposed to be a Light Worker. I needed some career guidance, fast. I didn't realize it at the time, but I found it by following a trail of crystal clear clues.

CHAPTER 9 　　　　　USING THE TOOLS

Be the change that you want to see in your life
　　　　　　　　　　　　　　～Mahatma Gandhi～

Jean-Pierre and I were having breakfast at a local hotel casino called the M Resort one morning in early 2009, when I started to hear what sounded like three voices in the distance. I stopped talking, tilted my head to the right and closed my eyes.

"What's wrong?" Jean-Pierre asked.

"Nothing," I replied, continuing without a hesitation that he would think I was mad. "I hear them talking, but I cannot quite grasp it. Shhh."

By this time, Jean-Pierre was getting used to this new type of conversation and was honoring it as the weirdness that was his wife since the perceived near-death experience. I wasn't sure if it amused him, or he was starting to believe it was possible for me to receive telepathic messages from beyond.

His answer was profound, "Stop listening with your ears and listen with your heart," he said. Then he went back to his breakfast.

"Wow, that was pure philosophical genius," I thought.

I discovered that this phenomenon is called clair-audience. I was learning a new psychic alphabet one day at a time in suburbia.

Sometimes, the messages sounded like Morse code, often occurring just as I was getting to fall asleep, beep, beep, bebeep. Some sharper tones, some longer, more pronounced frequency changes in my hearing. I would listen in as if the sounds were coming from outside of me.

"Someone is trying to reach me," I would jokingly tell Jean-Pierre. "I am getting Morse code in my ear."

As I was on the fast track learning about the awakening process of spirituality in my life, and the idea that we are spiritual beings having a physical experience to learn and gain wisdom, I became aware of our tonal quality that emanates from our being or frequency that we expel. It changes, increasing to a higher sound as we grow spiritually and gets closer to those on higher frequency planes or dimensions of existence. So, I chalked this up to shifts in vibration, or frequency changes, in the Universe, either being sent to the earth or those of higher frequency helping to raise mine.

You have to have a sense of humor about to not take yourself too seriously. Just like "coming out of the psychic closet," my friend Wendy used to say about our newly developed intuitive abilities. Not everyone you know will be okay with your newfound abilities or spiritual prowess. I learned the importance of being authentic, transparent, and true to myself by expressing it as a part of who I was becoming.

Another way of saying it is as humans, we are spiritual beings: energy in physical form using a human vehicle as a suit to get around. Everything is energy - we are energy, the desk you are writing on or the chair you are sitting in is energy - just different variations of frequency as with a variety of diverse radio stations.

In seeking the path of self-discovery and expansion, we remove lower vibrational energies from our existence, such as self-deprecating and demeaning thought, limiting talk, violence, and fear. As we replace these with higher vibrational practices by receiving energy healing such as Reiki, practicing meditation, listening to beautiful music, or being in nature, we start vibrating at faster, higher frequencies. Moving up to higher frequencies, you are no longer in alignment with certain things such as limiting habits and illness.

Everyone is intuitive and psychic. Everyone has healing abilities, but most of us do not activate these muscles or channels within ourselves or believe we can. The more work you do on yourself to raise your vibration and remove energy blockages, the more the intuitive channel is available to you. We are all special. As this vibrational change occurs, you start to drift away from people, places, and situations that you used to find comfortable without even a conscious thought as to why. You find the old conversations that you used to enjoy no longer hold value for you. Situations that used to be challenging somehow have an outcome that releases you from the burden. This is spiritual expansion at work.

You will learn to navigate using your "internal GPS," a term coined by Esther Hicks who channels a group consciousness known as Abraham. You may walk into a place of business and you feel amazing, because you have tapped into your heart and you may get chills of confirmation. Bingo! Do the deal. Understand the validation. Or, you meet someone who promises you a huge financial carrot, but you feel creepy. Move in another direction.

This is your guidance system giving you clues. I now call this the "Colander Effect". What no longer matches the new higher vibration falls out the holes of the colander – your life. Now, for those who might read this and think, higher vibration = good, lower vibration = bad, this is not a matter of judgment. It is just a different channel. As with a radio, there are different frequency channels that provide such options as Pop, Jazz, Blues, Rock and Roll and they do not judge each other. It is simply a personal choice for what feels good in your gut – a vibrational match.

In the weeks and months following my near-death experience, I was practicing conscious techniques to develop my internal GPS. I turned off the radio in the car and stopped watching television news and violent movies. It worked. Often, audible messages would come to me in the moments before sleep or in dreams. One morning I woke with a start, literally sat straight up, and shouted, "Iolite!" I jumped out of bed saying the word again and again, jotting it down before I would forget. Jean-Pierre was awake now looking at me oddly. I explained my dream.

"I was in some sort of classroom, and there were two beings helping me to remember something important so that when I woke up, I would not forget. They helped me with this by teaching me a little rhyming song." I sang a bit of the melody from my dream to Jean-Pierre.

"Iolite, you see the light..... lalalalal."

"How does he put up with me?" I thought, laughing on the inside. I went to my computer and typed in the strange unknown word "IOLITE," and there it was – a crystal! I read that one can use this bluish-purple or violet-colored stone during meditation to help induce the opening of the third-eye, the mystical concept associated with clairvoyant visions and inner knowing. Iolite is also believed to balance masculine and feminine energies.

I ran right out to find this Iolite, purchasing it at a local store in nearby Boulder City that sells crystals. I was so loving the treasure hunt aspect of the psychic guidance that was opening up. Just walking into the rock shop gave me pleasure. I could sense the energies of these stones. Their vibration.

I still remembered that day long ago, at the beginning of my journey, when I placed crystals under Jean-Pierre's pillow and prayed for a healing miracle. Now, in some strange way, maybe the crystals were answering my prayer. My destiny in the healing arts was still hidden. I needed guidance to find it.

It came literally in a flash of Reiki heat and light. One of our good friends was being certified as Reiki Level I, and Jean-Pierre and I were invited to the ceremony. Nine of us who regularly gathered for spiritual expansion at the time were guided to wash our hands in salt water and wiped them dry, as directed by our other friend, the Reiki Master. We sat on chairs in a circle. The energy in the room was amazing, full of love.

We all spoke about being able to feel the presence of non-physical beings in the room. There were candles and incense burning and appropriate background music to set a highly elevated mood. I watched as our friends, the Reiki Master and his girlfriend, presided over the ceremony. Moving his hand and index finger around our soon-to-be Reiki Level 1 certified friend as if writing in the air. It appeared to be a very private and personal experience between the Master and the initiate.

I am usually not big on ritual or ceremony in this manner, but somehow that seemed to change. Prior to my near-death experience and years before any awakening, I would have run out of this room. But this felt right and incredible. Jean-Pierre and I left first, as we needed to pick up Luke from the babysitter.

While riding in the car, I held up my hands, "Jean-Pierre, I have this tingling and heat in my hands. It's a strange feeling."

"You're making it up." was Jean-Pierre's response.

"How can I make up something like this, and why would I?" I replied. "I don't know how or why, but I feel this in my hands with this weird sensation like I have to keep them open and face up."

As we continued home, Jean-Pierre and I reviewed the ceremony and how the Reiki Master warned our friend who was being initiated that he would go through a cleansing process of his chakras that might lead to outbursts of emotion as he worked through blockages. The Master also explained that when you're working with energy, as in Reiki, you need to learn how to ground yourself, or you can "blow" your phone, or computer, or other electrical apparatus.

You couldn't script what happened next. We walked into our dark house, Jean-Pierre carrying a sleeping Luke in his arms. I reached for the bureau lamp to give him some light. I turned the switch and pop - the light bulb blew. I looked at Jean-Pierre in astonishment. We just laughed, but I had an inkling that something extraordinary was happening.

I woke up the next morning with exuberance. I had so much energy I nearly bolted out of bed. The sun was shining, and I was happy to be alive. Then, a shock. I was combing my wet hair in front of the mirror when I raked over the crown of my head. It was so sensitive, I flinched.

"What the heck! Why is the top of my head so sore?."

I touched it, felt a strange sensation of sensitivity and tingling. Then I remembered the Reiki Master touching my head during the ceremony as he was unusually guided to do to all who attended. My palms started tingling and heating up just then. This is incredible, I thought. My crown chakra has opened! I am not sure exactly what that means, but I just knew it. Phone calls to my Reiki friends brought confirmation.

"Apparently, Source was not going to wait for you to decide to become Reiki," a friend said. "They're going to help you along."

As I held my hands out, palms up as before, while still juggling the phone, I finally understood Maria's prediction that I would become a Light Worker. This is incredible! I was overwhelmed with excitement that I could feel such a physical manifestation.

"I need to learn Reiki. Will you teach me?" I asked my friend – one of the nine of our regular spiritual group.

One more telepathic message was coming to seal my commitment to practicing Reiki. Once again, crystals were my touchstone. One Saturday morning, I woke with an audible message from beyond: "There is a crystal you need to have."

I responded telepathically: "I can't spend any money on crystals right now. We can't pay the mortgage."

"It is on Craig's List," the messenger affirmed.

"No kidding." I laughed and gave in. "If there is a crystal on Craig's List, I will pursue it. Not promising, but I will pursue it."

I brushed my teeth, sat down at my computer in my nightie, and typed "crystals" in the search box on Craig's List for Las Vegas. Up popped a new entry as of that morning: "Crystals for Sale." And the location was in my neighborhood.

"Boy, you are good!" I offered with a vibrational pat on the non-physical back of my Spirit guide. The negotiation continued.

"Listen, I am not in a position to spend money on crystals right now," I advised. "However, I just returned an iron Mom gave me for Christmas from Target. The cash that I have is all I can spend on this crystal, and nothing more, if Jean-Pierre is okay with it. I really don't think it is a good idea to buy crystals right now."

But the telepathic suggestive urge was too strong. I had $50 in my wallet. "That should be more than enough," I thought. It was time to talk to Jean-Pierre. I gingerly approached his office, where he had begun to retreat more and more into video games, watching soccer online, or working on his photography. Jean-Pierre's office always reminded me of NASA West with all three of his computer monitors set up in an arch like some technology lab.

"Honey?" I said as melodically as possible. "There is something I need to discuss with you." Luke was off in another room playing, so I had Jean-Pierre's full attention.

"Sooo, I woke up with a message this morning," I said as he did not look up from his computers.

"Okaayyy," Jean-Pierre replied.

"I was told there is a crystal I need to buy," I continued.

Jean-Pierre swiveled around to look at me sternly. "When we have to move from this house, and we have nothing to live on but the crystals and rocks you have bought, I hope you will be satisfied," he said.

"Absolutely," I agreed. "I told them, No."

As I started to walk out of the room, he relented, saying, "You do what you are guided to do. I am not going to be the one who says no to something you are being guided to do." More and more, Jean-Pierre was showing less resistance for my new calling, and, for that, I was grateful.

I telephoned the woman who had posted on Craig's List. She and her husband were downsizing and had tables set up in their dining area displaying things they wanted to sell. There were 20-30 pieces of crystal and stones on display, ranging from palm-sized pieces to much larger ones. The only crystals I had purchased up to this time were small, tumbled stones that cost no more than a few dollars. This will be quick, I thought, as I picked up an inviting crystal, turned it over, and discovered a $300 price tag.

"Holy cow, this is way out of my league," I said aloud, not really meaning to be heard. The owner explained that this crystal was a "museum piece." As we continued to talk, I learned that she and her husband had traveled extensively, exploring the healing arts. Then she revealed that she was a Reiki Master. Ding!

Okay, there was a reason for this connection: Reiki to Reiki. We sat down at the kitchen table amongst crystals, and I explained the morning's message that had brought me here. She kindly allowed me a few minutes alone to look at the crystals and see which one I was guided to. I sat, heard the words "relax," "feel it," and "breathe." I closed my eyes, took a deep breath, opened them again and laid eyes on the most beautiful piece of royal blue stone I had ever seen. It had the graceful lines of the feminine form. I thought of the Blessed Mother Mary and the miracle of her visitation in my bedroom. I grabbed the stone in my right hand. Slowly, I turned this six-inch-tall natural sculpture over to reveal the price: $50. Unbelievable!

The owner, Marilyn, told me the stone was Lapis Lazuli and offered a crystal book with more information. The book explained that this stone had existed since before "time was born." Lapis Lazuli is believed to assist one in gaining admission to the domain of the unknown mysteries of sacred texts and esoteric ideas.

It is considered to be a 'stone of total awareness' with the power to assist one to expand their intuitive and psychic awareness. "Alrighty then," I said, as I pulled out my $50 and exchanged it for the stone in my hand. I was ready to journey forth.

After studying the Reiki manual, being guided by my Reiki Master, and going through the initiation attunements for Reiki Levels 1 and 2, I sent out a mass e-mail informing friends that I had become a Reiki practitioner. I wanted to practice, targeting around 30 sessions in two weeks. It was an incredible growth spurt for me. Prior to the near-death experience, I would have said, "not in a million years that my profession would be in healing arts." I loved it. It was natural and felt amazing.

"So, did you feel anything?" Jean-Pierre would jokingly accost our friends as they left the sessions in our home by way of the front door. I felt that Jean-Pierre wanted to believe, but he could not quite get past the cynicism. As my intuitive channel opened more and more, Jean-Pierre would joke, "Get any numbers?" referring to the lottery every time I would share with him some piece of extraordinary information that I received. "Get lottery numbers!" he would hint on a regular basis.

"I am not that kind of intuitive." I told him.

"You are if you want to be," he would sarcastically throw my advice back to me.

"I get information based on the spiritual needs of myself and people I come into contact with along my path," I told him. "It can be physical, emotional, or spiritual, but, so far, no numbers." I would tell my clients: "If you just met the man of your dreams, and you want to know if he is the one, I am not your intuitive healing practitioner. If you want to release the attachment of needing to know if he is the one, I am your gal."

Still, it was no wonder Jean-Pierre had numbers on his mind. Our finances were creeping toward disaster, he was becoming more paralyzed with his own fear and it wasn't clear how Reiki could come to our aid.

CHAPTER 10   THE GARDEN

The field of the soul must be watered by the rain with tears of love; otherwise it will become a desert

~Sorin Cerin~

I had newfound peace amid the chaos of my life. As one who has been gifted with the extraordinary experience of the dazzling contrast between these two realms, I must preface this chapter of our story with a word of advice, and, I hope, inspiration.

Life on earth cannot totally mirror the shining grace state of pure energy on the Other Side. As long as we live here on earth, we stand with our feet planted in two different worlds: the 3rd dimensional plane that allows us the education to expand our consciousness with lessons, and the higher planes that offer us the guidance to maneuver these obstacles to the highest and best outcome for our soul's education. We may struggle with obstacles, both external and internal. Sometimes, we stumble; sometimes, we ignore the guidance or the signs.

I suppose there is no changing this condition until we evolve, pass over, or become enlightened. Enlightenment is not a term I use for my experience, as it connotes some highly-elevated state of being that I have not reached. However, the state of searching is my personal journey and connection to my Creator and Source, not for perfection, but perfectibility. I am in a state of awakening along my spiritual path and purpose. As I discovered next, as long as we are searching, we are finding our destiny. Expect the process to be messy, challenging, and sometimes, even heartbreaking. But always, the great victory of Spirit is within grasp moment by moment if we allow it to be so.

For Jean-Pierre and me, the challenge of 2009, as I embarked on my new career as a Reiki practitioner, centered on our home finances. The almighty house of worry on Kagen Circle towered over us.

What happened to my home, my sanctuary, my dream, the life that started with such promise with Jean-Pierre? Jean-Pierre's court case settled, and, although the reward was sustaining us during this time, it certainly was not overflowing, nor was it worth the price paid – my husband – our marriage. Like so many other families riding the downside of the real estate meltdown, our mortgage was significantly underwater, and we were drowning.

After the bank refused to modify the mortgage, we sought legal advice. Then we made the drastic decision to stop paying our mortgage as was advised by the bank, in hopes that the bank would reconsider and work with us. "We cannot talk to you until you are not current." How absurd! It was a radical strategy in a crazy system, but it appeared to be our only option to keep the house.

Now, with every unpaid mortgage, we fell thousands of dollars more in arrears. The idea of ever bringing the loan current was now a buried hope. Foreclosure notices appeared on our door, and the postman brought certified letters from the bank on a regular basis. The foreclosure "monster" haunted us by day and in our dreams at night. We were so afraid to lose our home, but understanding it was inevitable, the embarrassing stigma slowly was fading.

Meanwhile, Mom was now showing signs of failing

health – mostly forgetfulness. By the time I embarked on the marathon Reiki practice sessions in our home, Mom had suffered two frightening episodes when she was not been sure where she was: one at the shopping mall with me, and the other when she was in a taxi and was not able to tell the driver where she lived.

It was so sad to see her this way, as I had always known my mother to be "sharp as a tack."

In between these episodes she was incredibly lucid and clear, never a glimpse that there was something wrong, as if there were a blip on the timeline. Sometimes now she would forget to shut off the water kettle or a pot on the stove. If we were not home, we might arrive to a smoky, burnt smell in the house, and find Mom trying to clear out the aftermath with fans blowing and doors wide open. We bought an electric kettle, and that solved the problem for a while. We tried to coach her.

"Mom, please do not leave the kitchen when you have something on the stove. Really, you could burn the house down. Is that phone call really that important?" To her, a ringing phone was what she lived for. It took precedent over eating, cooking, or being in the middle of a conversation.

The emergency room doctor diagnosed her first episode as a mini-stroke. Subsequent doctors confirmed that with Mom's significantly blocked carotid artery, this was very possible. They advised that this could lead to forgetfulness and, in time, dementia.

Each time we visited doctors, Mom would ignore the advice or the medicine as there were side effects with each that she was not willing to accept, including taking a baby aspirin. She was often indignant. We never got anywhere except more appointments.

Behind the scenes, this was the not-so-peaceful backdrop of my Reiki practice marathon for friends in April, 2009. After a couple of weeks of sequestering my husband and my mother in their respective rooms while I performed Reiki sessions for friends in my dining room (turned office, turned Reiki room), it was time to look for a real office.

I left the house early one spring morning in 2009 with the mission of finding a place to work without having to pay outright rent. A shared environment with perhaps a percentage split would be optimal. I waited for guidance. With Luke in preschool, I kissed Jean-Pierre and Mom goodbye and headed out the door to a fading bellow from Jean-Pierre: "Don't spend any money!"

On the first day of my search, my internal GPS led me to an oasis in the desert. A sweet village-style setting with 30 one-story office buildings. Within an hour, a lease was negotiated for two rooms with brilliant tenant-friendly terms. My new Reiki practice and meditation center was being delivered before my eyes. In telepathic messages that same day, Spirit guides laid out the vision of my Reiki future.

The grandeur of it was overwhelming. I felt dwarfed by the vision.

"How will I accomplish this?" I asked.

"We will guide you." The messengers replied.

"Why me?"

"There are many to whom the message was sent, but not all will answer." They added.

"How can I do this by myself"

"You won't."

The messengers added: "Remember this guidance; it is extremely important. First: Everyone you will ever need will be guided to you - students, practitioners, and instructors, as well as helpers. Just ask for help. Second: Have fun! This is a gift for you. Remember balance. Third: Get out of the way!"

Within two weeks, I was shown how easily life can be lived when you follow and allow the flow of creation to work. I call this flow being in the "Slipstream." Your day unfolds like a well-orchestrated play. All joyful experiences and all the solutions to perceived complications just flow. It takes far less effort to maneuver your life, and life becomes more peaceful, joyful, love-filled, and just plain fun.

You are in the moment-by-moment ride of your life. Bliss is something that is part of your day, even if the world around you would judge your circumstances as challenging, difficult or even traumatic. You are in the "Slipstream." The Universe is giving you back exactly what you are creating. Then, what you create is more in alignment with what you want, and the life that was challenging becomes the life you love.

It's seems easy, no? Yes, it can be. It is amazing how challenging it can be to get there and STAY there. I became acutely aware of everyone's role in this process, and it helped me understand soul groups a bit better - the idea that we reincarnate in soul groups to assist each other, sometimes all through our lives, and sometimes at specific times. I learned to acknowledge these souls for the gifts that they provided, both joyful and painful, as with each was enormous growth. Manifestations were everywhere. As I established my practice, called Reiki by Lee, people were just showing up with little effort in marketing. Teachers, clients, and students quickly found my hideaway in the office park tucked at the far end with no street sign. It was time to step up my personal network and have an opening party inviting my sphere of contacts.

My friend, Paul Isensee, came to the Open House and showered me with such affection, my heart overflowed.

"I love what you are doing, and, if there is anything I can do to help you, just ask," he offered as we said our goodbyes.

It was hard for me to ask for help, but I knew this was part of the lesson. The business part of me was starting to overpower the balance in my life to move this Reiki practice into a viable profession which actually produced an income. I was managing and healing the limited belief that to be in service meant that I needed to be poor.

I remember my mother teaching me as a young girl, "Pay your own way and you will always be welcome." That flowed into don't be a burden by asking for anything. Paul and I joke about how well I have overcome that belief and how that innocent initial offer to help led to him working at the center on evenings and weekends. As we continued to open up more treatment and classrooms, Paul worked full-time and stepped into the role of my business partner.

He immediately connected to the vision for the center as a mission, not as a business opportunity. He jumped in knowing I was using all the income to grow the center, not on salaries, as the mission of light needed it to be a particular and significant size by 2011, marking a time of great transition and the need for such a large center.

Paul and I work so well together, we have come to realize that we have done this journey before in previous lives. An intuitive channel revealed that Paul and I had been in the prehistoric lost civilization of Atlantis together running a school. I am most grateful that this talented Spirit agreed to take this ride with me once again.

And what a spectacular ride 2009 had been. Only the ticking of the clock, toward the day when Jean-Pierre and I, Luke, and Mom might not have our home, cast a shadow on the year. As it drew to a close, I had one of the strangest dreams of my life. Mom, Delphine, and I were at the home in Maryland where I grew up. We were all looking up at the sky, and it was changing as we were watching it. All of us eyes to the skies watched intently.

The sky was getting bigger and opening up as if to reveal the backstage of a play as though this world were just an illusion, and the wrapping, as if it were a gift, was being opened up to show something else beyond the sky. The moon was large and full, and God's hand held the moon. Large killer whales, black and white, came flying across the sky and then dipped down to kiss each one of us. The Angel of Death dropped into the dream. Suddenly, all of us were sitting together in a car.

"Are you here to take Mom?" I asked.

"No, I am here for you," the Angel of Death replied. He appeared to be very sad, and I asked him why he was so very upset. "The state of the world," he said. The dream did not prove to be prophetic, or even to contain any clear guided message. But I connected to the dream's cosmic darkness, and the feeling of dread stayed with me for days. I have since learned there is a significant symbolism

117

surrounding Orcas or Killer Whales and that is one of cosmic journey, spirituality and healing.

Now that we had stopped paying our mortgage, I have to admit our owner pride was waning for a house we no longer owned, and spending money on it to keep it in good repair seemed a waste of funds. This once vibrantly cared-for property was showing signs of deterioration and the lack of love was showing, just as the degrading marriage was also showing signs. We were slowly letting go of our future here, as we released our service providers one by one. From the house cleaner, landscaper to window washer, our home was being degraded to a house. That made the next telepathic guidance I received all the more intriguing. My Spirit guides instructed me to plant a garden in the house we were going to lose any day!

The message was triggered by my discovery of a book called The Square-Foot Garden, which outlined a concept of above ground organic gardening which is great in areas that do not have productive soil. This is certainly the case in Vegas. The concept is to use densely populated plants in above ground, sectioned-off, square-foot areas. It sounded perfect for me, as I adore squares and things organized neatly in straight-line designs. I am not a fluid line person. Virgos need structure.

I attacked the square-foot garden project as this bull-headed gal from Czech/Pole descent only would. Jean-Pierre remained consistently skeptical.

"You are going to go through all this work and expense, and we will not even be here to reap the rewards," he predicted. "We will have to hop the wall to pick a tomato," he added.

It didn't deter me, as I learned guided messages were not to be ignored. The expense was minimal. Friends offered their truck, and I headed to Home Depot. There, amazingly, the clerk who quickly filled my lumber order was so inexplicably taken with the project concept, he offered to build free of charge the needed four-by-four-foot above ground squares from the lumber I had purchased. I could pick them up the next day. I was in the "Slipstream," and I loved Home Depot!

The rest of the process ran with the same precision and flow in the planting season that fall of 2009. With assistance from Jean-Pierre, who was gradually on board, friends and neighbors, the six above ground garden beds went up, filled with a combination of mulch and topsoil, planted with various seeds.

We had no automatic irrigation, so every morning Jean-Pierre or I would go out to these six garden beds and water them with a hose. It was therapeutic and exciting to watch the sprouts of life coming from the rich soil. It was also great to allow Luke to see how miraculous a garden can be. We were amazingly still in our house, though Jean-Pierre had urged me to pack months ago.

"Lee, this is not something we can do in a couple of days," he said. "There is so much stuff to pack here."

I declined, explaining that if I packed, I would be telling the Universe I was ready to go. And I was not. I had just started Reiki by Lee and was not feeling the guidance to focus on anything else but spiritual healing practices. The task was also overwhelming, and the idea of packing up around Mom was not something I relished, either. It would have stressed her completely and I was not sure of the impact it would have on her.

Additionally, I knew I would get a message when it was time. Jean-Pierre was angry and frustrated with me. One early morning, I was out in the backyard watering our little plant babies in my nightie, in the same manner I usually watered ... counting to 10 in each square. "1,2,3,4,5,6,7,8,9,10 ... Next square ... 1,2,3,4,5,6,7,8,9,10 ... Next square.

Then: "Stop!" I heard, as if someone were next to my ear. I whipped around to see who was in the backyard. No one.

"What?" I said audibly

"Stop counting," said the voice.

"Seriously?"

"Yes. Stop counting and feel the water. Feel the plants."

One of my Spirit guides was presenting a new lesson plan, a challenging one. I had spent 40-some years doing things a certain way, and now I was being taught to use a new muscle, my intuition, my feelings, in a new way. In the first square I was still counting but, by the sixth square, I was feeling the water and listening to my inner knowing of when to stop. Closing my eyes and then opening one eye to see if it was over-watered, I was practicing and using this new muscle. I was getting the hang of this.

The voice returned: "You know we did not guide you to plant this garden to reap the rewards of its fruit."

"No?" I questioned silently and telepathically to my non-physical friends that now felt like a group consciousness rather than a single voice.

"No, it was an answer to your prayer." This practice of group consciousness felt like the same kind of guidance I had when those Light Beings connected during my near-death experience.

"What prayer?" I asked,

"The prayer to keep your house," they answered.

"Huh?" I thought.

"You see, we guided you to plant roots here. You will be able to stay while you get your footing."

Wow, this was an amazing encounter. Do I tell Jean-Pierre, or do I sit with this one awhile? I decided to wait.

About a month went by, and Jean-Pierre's stress was rising. He felt that he needed to carry all the worry for the family because I had given up worrying. It was hard to witness, but I also knew there was nothing I could do to release this for him. We all have to come to that space on our own, the futility of worry. I could no longer jump on board that worry wagon like I used to.

"We need to pack," Jean-Pierre again urged me, starting with a calm tone. "I have gotten another notice, actually 30 of them, as they send you by certified mail every variation of your name, and mine, and our trust. They want us out, and the house is going into foreclosure. We have a couple of weeks."

Again, I declined. I just knew that the Universe would not ask me to take on this mission of starting a Reiki center and guiding me to my life path and then kick us out on the street with Luke and Mom in tow. And also, that garden message was clear.

"Nope, not gonna pack."

A couple of weeks later, I came in the house from watering the new garden. Jean-Pierre said that something extraordinary had happened. Our dear friend Adam had offered to put a contract on the house. If accepted, we could rent back from him so that we would not have to leave, and Mom would not be moved, either.

An extraordinary offer, indeed, and friend! This was the moment I had been waiting for.

"Jean-Pierre, there is an experience I had in the garden that I want to tell you about..."

CHAPTER 11   DIFFERENT PERSPECTIVES

What you think and what you feel and what you manifest is always a match, every single time, no exceptions

~Esther Hicks-Abraham~

By the fifth year my mother had lived with us, the challenges of this elderly person in the house were prominent. There were glimmers of happiness for Mom that mostly revolved around our son Luke, but she was depressed, lonely, and insecure, just as she had been when she lived in Baltimore. The shocking gap between Mom's reality and mine came crashing down one day in 2010 when I was working in the house. I knew Mom was on the phone, as she often was, but I never paid attention to what she was saying – until this day.

Now I overheard my mother telling someone how horrible her life was in our home. She described an existence that was so far from the truth, and I was totally crushed. It was a punch to my very soul that took my breath away. It completely and totally shattered me. I cried harder than I could remember doing for a long time. Jean-Pierre found me and asked what was going on.

Through the hysteria, I got out that I had overheard her saying how unfairly she was being treated, being left home all the time, yelled at "all the time" by Jean-Pierre and me, and not cared for.

It was unimaginable for me to hear this. We had eagerly opened our home and changed the trajectory of our lives for my mother in hopes of giving her a platform for an amazing expression of her later years. We cooked for her daily, coddled her, loved her, scheduled and took her to her many doctors' visits, nail and hair appointments, entertained, shopped with her, and supported her emotionally when there were issues to be addressed and spoiled her in many ways because we wanted to. We always made her a priority in our lives and shared our family. We gave up our privacy and our intimacy for her. Her words were untrue and cruel.

What had happened? My mother had become hard for me to read. I pondered whether her cruel streak was due to old age. But the reality of those words coming from my mother's mouth made it hard to conceive that it wasn't really her. Could something in her brain be telling her some other reality or was this really her? One moment she would be lucid and clear in her conversations, and we would be connecting beautifully just like the old days, and the next it was like playing a game of charades to try to decipher what she was trying to say.

"You know that round thing that has cheese on it,"

"You mean pizza, Ma?"

It was not only the helplessness of dementia, but also the progression of a person in their elder years becoming more of who they are. Perhaps it was a lack of will to hide her less appealing traits, or just a relaxed state of being in the truth of who she was.

For my Mom, growing old was a double-edged sword: petrified to die but despising the process of aging. We differed in this as well. As she complained of wrinkles and belly fat in her 80's, I vowed to never become so attached to the physical for this to develop in me and to cherish my older years with the wisdom that only age can bring. I would try to assist Mom with this by telling her jokes about aging or inspirational quotes, like Nobody grows old merely by living a number of years. We grow old by deserting our ideals. Years may wrinkle the skin, but to give up enthusiasm wrinkles the soul. by Samuel Ullmannot. She would chuckle or dismiss it as if she had no interest in changing her thoughts.

Mom began seeping deeper into the secretive nature that she had always had. In the past, I had been the one person she shared her secrets with, her co-conspirator, or so I believed, as if we had an invisible secret handshake. She started shutting me out.

I would have never believed this would be possible. Life with Mom became an unconscious game designed to keep me guessing. This seemingly sweet and generous soul was so desperately starved for attention, she would use manipulation as a means to feed her need by any means. I would see glimpses of the mother I knew and I was right back in her graces, and I loved the warmth of this space.

Then, Mom would tell me something, but she would add, "Don't tell Jean-Pierre." Now I realized I had actually done this with her my entire life, as if it were perfectly acceptable behavior. "Don't tell Dad," she would say. Or, "Don't tell your sister." In past years, I had run interference between Mom and every person whom she had an issue with. But it was exhausting and energetically very debilitating. It was a constant game of cat and mouse, and the will to continue was proving that I was going to be the one to get eaten.

However, I had changed. I was working extensively on changing myself to a more authentic person, raising my vibration, and working through blockages of past negative learned behaviors such as, not being pulled into negative talk or drama activators. After my near-death experience, I was not falling for the game.

"Mom, if you have something to tell me and I cannot share it with my husband, then please do not tell me," I would say. Maybe that is when things started changing between us in a bigger way.

The phone conversation I overheard shook me deeply. It shattered me. Afterward, I found it difficult to "like" my mother. I loved her for sure. I appreciated the enormous sacrifices she had made for us children. I was immensely grateful for her emotional and financial support. I cherished the positive influences she provided with respect to her huge capacity to love our son and be there for those in need, but I no longer "liked" her the way I used to like her. The depth of the stab was too damaging.

My alienation from her grew as I learned about more secret tales of neglect she had told family members and friends. I discovered that she would have long and ongoing conversations with our neighbor, fabricating stories with the intent of producing sympathy. As the mother-related drama escalated, there was no hiding from the truth. I had to honor that my mother was not happy and she was having a significant impact on my family life and my health.

I admit that fleetingly, I actually wanted to get back in her good graces, but I knew that would be too high a price to pay. The day had come to be true to myself and my family. Following an episode where Mom flooded our laundry room, and a subsequent doctor's visit for me that showed enormous stress-related health issues, it was time. After accompanying Mom to another of many of her doctor's appointments, I spent the time in the car ride home in a complete stupor. She was talking non-stop about the health issues of my eldest sister and how she wanted to find an answer for her, but she had not considered the recent news of my ill health significant enough for mention. I reached my breaking point.

"I am tired, Mom," I said calmly. "I cannot do this anymore. You are unhappy with us, and all our efforts are never good enough. I think you should move back East."

This did not come completely out of the blue, as I had started to discuss the possibility with Delphine. She was aware of how unhappy Mom was, as she was one of the new confidantes. Little did she know that being the confidant doesn't mean that she receives the truth. Delphine was amazingly supportive during this time, understanding the depth of emotional toll the past six years had taken.

"It is my turn now," she said.

Jean-Pierre was deeply hurt because at the end of Mom's time with us, before she moved back to Baltimore, he became the scapegoat. She wouldn't even look at him. The details of any reasoning were never really identified, except that she told others that Jean-Pierre was the reason she was being "kicked out." Even though it was my complete decision, and I had instigated it, he was the one at whom she pointed all the blame. Again, using the phone as a personal lifeline to detail her distorted version of the story, she shared more tales of unhappiness. I tried to give solace to Jean-Pierre, explaining that no one is immune to the vitriolic attacks from my mother. Now he should truly feel like part of the family.

"How do I get past this?" I wondered. "How do I heal from this?" I listened to my internal knowing for guidance. It was the hardest decision of my life. If Mom was not going to flourish here, and our lives were being impacted so deeply, I felt like I had to do something. Otherwise, I was offering us all up to destruction as a family. Was it even too late? Was the damage done?

It was time to take the authentic step of honoring Jean-Pierre and Luke, and showing the Universe this behavior is not acceptable in my life. Delphine found a lovely facility for seniors in Baltimore with lush grounds and upgraded amenities. I called it the Ritz Carlton of senior facilities. Mom's savings would carry her through there in style. Maybe Mom would finally be happy there amongst her peers and back with those who suggested that we should have never moved her.

I flew Mom back to Baltimore, and Delphine and I got her settled into her new home. We kept it positive as an exciting adventure, which is what we do really well, Delphine and I. Mom was sad to leave the house, and especially Luke, and Jean-Pierre was his normal respectful and loving self, saying our goodbyes at the airport. But, of course, there was an underlying layer of trepidation and sadness during the week I spent there. I would return to Vegas to pack up the rest of Mom's things, now that I had experienced how much room she had, and her key furniture pieces and remaining clothes would be packed up and sent by movers.

The day I was leaving, I sat in my rental car feeling like I was leaving my child at boarding school. Despite the choice I had made to send her back East, and the disabling hurt that I was experiencing from what I had come to learn about Mom, in that moment, I wanted to swoop her up and carry her away to somewhere safe. It wasn't rational, but it was what I felt. I momentarily felt a reversal of roles and remembered when Mom had left me at first grade and literally had a tug-of-war over me with the nun.

The anger, resentment, and betrayal that welled in me from the deepest parts of my being was almost more than I could bear, but I had the tools now. I realized that my part in this scenario was that I unfairly elevated my mother as some saint. For many years, I associated her with a lofty view but, in reality, she was just a soul like all of us, challenged with layers of emotional peeling to be done. For Mom, her fears, worries, jealousies, lack of self-confidence, holding grudges, and lack of awareness of her true connection to God were areas that I could not assist, as hard as I tried. Her journey, her lessons!

In the months that passed after we moved Mom to Baltimore, the soul searching led me to clarity. I learned I did not need a confidante, because my life was no longer confidential. I no longer needed a rescuer, because there is no need for rescuing when you rely on your own connection to Source and create your own reality. I was different, and that was not her fault. I could not blame her, as there was nothing to blame. There was only my part in the play. In this exploration, I found a new appreciation for this woman and for her life as my mother.

For nearly 40 years, I held her in the highest possible esteem. Being tagged as "the favorite" from my sisters, I grew up with a sense of being special in my mother's eyes. I was the youngest, I was the most like my mother, and I was her die-hard companion. How could all that change in just a few years of living together? But it did.

I came to the place of greater compassion that the Blessed Mother had urged me to provide. I would show my mother and my family this compassion and the courage it took to move Mom back to where she needed to be for that connection to solidify. Our relationship mended while Mom was living in her new apartment, and we went back to our telephone conversations.

One day, I hope that we will be able to review this journey of ours together, like my life review took me through. We will telepathically talk it through together in the early morning over a cup of coffee as my mother so loved in her earlier days. The Other Side will provide a fresh and enlightened perspective, with immense love and without the attachment we experienced in this life.

CHAPTER 12   THE AWAKENING

Life does not limit you! Opulence does not limit you!
Love does not limit you! Therefore, why allow your
human limiting concepts to bind you longer?

                              ~Master St. Germain~

Reiki by Lee was growing by leaps and bounds; we reached the milestone of 100 members which gave Paul and me such satisfaction. Later, we counted over 800 members in 2011. When I had been given the mission to open the center, I was petrified. It took a lot of convincing on the part of my guidance, and yet, somewhere inside me, no convincing at all was needed.

I know that might not make sense, but those early days were full of contradictions in feelings, of excitement and possibility, fear and anxiety.

What I realize is that with each little shift, I have grown enormously. The first year of Reiki by Lee was painful. I will not sugarcoat it. With all the guidance and all the assistance and support by loved ones and non-physicals, it was excruciating at times, as I released emotional blocks and continued to doubt the road I was traveling. I felt as if I were five years old wearing my mother's shoes, and I could not manage to walk without clomping down the hall and falling every few steps. Dealing with fear, ego, judgment, self-doubt, trust, and, did I say, fear was on my daily to-do list. It was not only my fear but what I was experiencing as a mirror from others. Seeing these issues play out in other people was a guide for me to grow. I was having situations volleyed up at every turn providing me another opportunity for expansion.

I cried a lot! And released a lot!

I was given a tremendous gift to evaluate myself as the main character of each of the short stories unfolding around me. From these, I could glean jewels of clarity that assisted me in realizing that all these diverse issues were reflections of me. As I slowly let go of them, they let go of me. I peeled away and released layer upon layer of the proverbial onion that was the "gunk" of my emotional self. As I worked through these barriers, I became emotionally and spiritually stronger; open to the higher vibration of Source Light.

The healing processes for me and others were spectacular. I continue to be in awe of the beauty and power of the Creator. I am humbled by what is possible. The more I spend time in Las Vegas, the more I adore it. With all that is said about it being Sin City, being a spiritual vortex is almost certainly not what you have heard. But it is true. There has always been a heart to Las Vegas ... a Soul for that matter.

It is bustling with world-renowned talent, incredible architecture when you know where to go, and amazing art collections, terrific off-Strip music locales that offer exceptional singing talent, exquisite restaurants, and breathtaking nature. Of course, what you mostly hear about is what draws approximately 40 million visitors a year: the casinos. And yes, you can find beauty even in the casinos if you want to see it.

From the lights, interiors, landscape and retail windows to the laughter and excitement that is present. For the most part, people are having fun! That is deeply soulful. It is all about the perspective, isn't it? There is the opposite of this, but that is what makes contrast. And contrast is grand.

But can it be said that Las Vegas is spiritual? Yes. The City of Sin has been transforming ever so subtly behind the scenes into the most amazing spiritual hub. It is alive with an abundance of spiritual and metaphysical seekers who offer classes, group meetings, alternative healthcare modalities, and personal coaching on a daily basis. If you were coming to Vegas on a holiday or convention, you might never know this subculture exists on the wings of The Strip.

Of course, there are variables that can come into play in this kind of evaluation, such as what constitutes "Spiritual." I am talking beyond religion or churches - groups of people gathering for the sole purpose of expanding themselves spiritually by connecting with Source - meditating, reading, listening to devotional music, or just gathering to discuss consciousness expansion.

So, what brings all of these spiritual people to the gambling capital of the world, a place that many outsiders believe to be an infertile desert void of depth? Is it a new job? A family member in need? Maybe at one time, the low cost of housing? An invitation by a friend? The weather?

I have found, in my experience over the years I have lived in Vegas, that people were guided here for a purpose … possibly a purpose of higher vibration. Maybe it was that Vegas needed to raise the spiritual quotient. The old nickname and tagline, "What Happens in Vegas Stays in Vegas" is one the town has embraced and marketed enthusiastically, which targets a hedonistic demographic. However, this city, and those who reside and visit here, understand it is being transformed into a rich stream of abundant self-realization.

Some would probably say that the extreme dissimilarity between Las Vegas, adult playground, and the idea of the same city being a spiritual go-to place, is ridiculous. I say, it's perfect.

Why do people link Love & Hate together, Light & Dark, Hot & Cold, and Sweet & Tart? Contrast! Yes, the beauty of contrast. It is our friend to be embraced if we choose it. For example, if I am in a cold, dark room, feeling chilled to the bone and fearful that I cannot see, when I experience the warmth and illumination of sunlight, how joyful I will be. Using the same idea, suppose I am in a city that is known for overindulgence, legal controversy, and morally questionable behaviors, which may lead to dark emotions such as regret, shame, and fear. But then I find a welcoming, supportive, genuine light shining bright like a beacon to find my way home through spiritual centers and communities. Doesn't that contrast apply to those who are seeking relief?

"Contrast is not about something going wrong. Nothing ever goes wrong, because every piece of contrast, no matter how wrong it seems to be, is always helping you to clarify what it is you do want." Is a quote from ABRAHAM, Group Consciousness channeled by Esther Hicks. With that being said, Las Vegas, in all its contrast, is prime for a transformation.

Does the idea of going to a spiritual center or community make you squeamish? It once did for me. It reeked of holy-roller or "woo woo," and I was not comfortable with either. For me, it conjured up all sorts of religious or cult associations too far out of my comfort zone, the feelings deep in my psyche. Join a group? No way! They may make me hug strangers or chant or hold hands. Okay, there are still churches and groups that do this, but that is wonderful because that attracts the people that want this kind of connection. And, I must confess, I am now a hugger and have been known to chant.

When you find yourself expanding your consciousness and heart, hugging and chanting just might feel comfortable to you one day. The beauty is that you seek what makes you comfortable, and feel good at every stop along the self-realized road. When I opened Reiki by Lee, I was clear that it must be a professional environment, a new breed of spiritual center - a professional, open, comfortable place for individuals who have, for whatever reason, moved away from their organized religion in search of a broader awareness of a combined unity. Or, people who needed a place to add to their spiritual practice that was not associated with any religion, but honored all.

We coined the phrase "living center" to express this purpose. We intended to create an amalgamation of wellness center and spiritual center for this new transitioning time of awakening. The goal of a living center is to provide a foundation to assist searchers on their individual journeys to higher consciousness – a supportive place to clear energy blockages in an effort to find peace within and better health and wellbeing based on their own internal guidance.

Sometime in our second year, I had a lucid dream about it being time to give our expanding living center a new name. I was urged to wake up and write it down. I did not. I awoke knowing it would begin with the "Ga" sound and end with "a." Over months of asking and no response, the missing piece leaped out at me in a gift shop at a California meditation retreat center called the Self Realization Center. Ganesha is the Hindu Deity known for overcoming obstacles.

That was it! What could be a more perfect name for a spiritual center during these trying times for so many? Reiki by Lee became Ganesha Center in early 2010, serving people at all stages of their spiritual path, all walks of life, age groups, gender, and preferences. Soul City - Las Vegas was now a reality, and we were right in the middle of it.

It was time to share this remarkable story. I had been urged by my guides to start writing the book that would detail my journey. When did I have time? So, I pushed it off. Not until I met Sharon Bridwell, a channel like I have never experienced before, did I get the "kick in the pants" to get started. There are many channels these days, as it is quite possible for everyone to open up their intuitive nature to channel higher beings. But this unassuming and God-loving soul is special indeed.

The sign marker occurred the night before I met Sharon while I was typing an email to a new acquaintance, a gal who interviewed me for her online spiritual travel log. As I was closing the email, I heard the word "flower" in my consciousness, as if it were the name I should use to address Lilou Mace, the interviewer. I adored her, but we were just meeting and it would be too familiar a nickname.

"Wow, that was weird," I thought. I actually typed the name as guided and then thought better of it and hit delete. "Okay, I am not going to call a girl that I just met, Flower." I thought. The following day, I met Sharon. Our meeting went longer than I had expected. As we talked, she shared with me that she channels Ascended Masters – certain enlightened humans reincarnated as higher beings, according to the teachings of Theosophy.

She also revealed that she channels her great grandmother, who calls her "Flower." I nearly fell off my chair. What a marker! I knew Sharon was going to be important, and she has been. She is a spiritual sister. I have been on the receiving end of many channels. My skepticism radar is always on high, but it took just 3 sentences from Sharon's great grandmother to blow me away with accuracy.

Most astonishing was her insight into the book my guides had been prodding me to write for a year. Up until now, pressing matters like running the center, my Reiki practice and, of course, my family had consumed every minute of my time. The urge to start writing was getting stronger by the month, but I couldn't see clear to carve out the time.

It can be quite an undertaking to write a book. I know people who have done it, and it was all-consuming. Sharon had no idea that I was thinking about this book project. But now, in May 2011, Great Grandmother, through Sharon, began to describe a specific location.

"You are near a river, with very tall evergreen trees and greenery," Great Grandmother said. "You are reading...no, you are writing...you are writing a book."

I was astonished. Great Grandmother's description was a perfect match to a place I had visited just a year before when Jean-Pierre, Luke, and I took a trip to Three Rivers, California, just outside Sequoia National Park. I had told Jean-Pierre "no camping" and, in Jean-Pierre style, he uncovered the most glorious refuge. I fell in love with the quaint Rio Sierra Riverhouse and its owner, Mars Roberts.

I knew immediately that the connection to the inn and Mars was more significant than the initial meeting. Rio Sierra was one of those incredible gems that Jean-Pierre has an uncanny ability to find. I was in heaven. The property is right on a raging river and, as Mars allowed us to tour the vacant rooms before new guests arrived, I found myself dreaming of writing my book here - all in Divine timing. Now, almost a year later, Great Grandmother was describing in detail the exact place where I was to write, and that place was Rio Sierra Riverhouse.

This was a message to get in gear and contact Mars. After detailing this extraordinary experience with Sharon and the description of Rio Sierra, I took the leap of faith and called Mars to schedule coming to California to start my book. Heading off to this special spot, I was filled with anticipation of a much-needed rest and some quiet time to write. I was enjoying the six-hour drive with Jean-Pierre in his 4 Runner in front of me, and Luke with me in my Volvo, heading for the beautiful and quaint area of Three Rivers.

As a first-time author, my Spirit guides told me that I would detail my experiences with my own awakening, with a section that written with additional assistance. Perhaps this meant I would channel this material, I felt, without really knowing. I had never knowingly channeled before.

Jean-Pierre spent the weekend with us before heading back to Las Vegas to pick up his work shift for Monday. This was a difficult time for us because Jean-Pierre's new job was driving a taxi, and it was horrific. The shift was 4 a.m. to 4 p.m., which meant that Jean-Pierre would wake up at 2 a.m. and spend all day in a car, which was not helpful for his back or for getting any exercise. Most passengers treated him like a low-class citizen; he would sometimes get a 10-cent tip or none at all.

The deterioration of his self-esteem and zest for life plummeted. They work you so hard, with so little time off, that it leaves you no time to look for other work. It was a rat race that was taking its toll on him by the day. He had no joy and no patience, even worse than before.

I settled in on my first day of writing, with Luke being amazing and playing on his own in the room. Then something extraordinary occurred: a drop-in visitation by a Spirit presence, just as the Spirit guides had told me would happen. I heard this Spirit with my clairaudient knowing.

He said: "My name is Joseph, and I am going to be your helper for the book. The last chapter will be from me." This Spirit sent forth the most powerful energy I have yet experienced.

"Okay," I agreed. I was excited. I wanted to get finished so that I could get to the last chapter.

A few nights later, when Luke was asleep, the Spirit Joseph came to me again, I cleared my thoughts and asked that my vibration be lifted to match a good connection with Joseph. My fingers started moving fast around the keyboard. I was conscious that I needed to type fast to keep up with the thoughts Joseph was dropping into my consciousness.

These are Joseph's words, from June 15, 2011:

Love enters us from a well of existence that is streaming from the natural Source. We do not own it; it flows freely and is given with no requirement or judgment of its use. It is the life force of all creation.

I am here to tell you that this life force runs through each and every one of you, and each and every one of all living beings in the cosmos. If you could glimpse for just one moment, the purity of the light of all existence - the same moment that we allowed Lee to experience and to draw upon for her strength in her journey as she continues to expand into the being that she already is - it would most definitely change you.

The worry and the fear that penetrates every layer of your current existence would vanish like a streak of lightening in the night sky. It would melt all the worry and darkness from your hearts and fill you with the light of love for all mankind.

There would be no differences, no wars to fight, no burdens of finance, as with this love, all things for all people are possible.

Your limited knowing of what the light is, is the only problem or issue that you need to resolve. The only issue. As once this clarity is yours, you will no longer seek anything but the essence that is the light of pure energy. You see, the strength that is the YOU that you do not know is just below the surface to be uncovered by you. This is the journey, you see.

It is the unveiling of the shell that you have encrusted upon yourself in darkness so that you can see again. The world is your playground, your playhouse, your school. It is that for each and every one of you.

Some of you see now, and some of you are beginning to see. It is a joyous occasion for all of those who are able to see this unfold. It is glorious in many ways, as your existence is unfolding in the hands of those who seek. You are the beauty and the life of all beings and all people, and the sages of the old ways will no longer be the ones that those follow, as the followers will be only you in your own path of seeking. This is true for all. Do not seek to find what is already within you. The path to the enlightened is with you.

I was blown away by the energy that was flowing through me. There was a lull in the download. "Is there anything else?" I asked. "This was very good for our first time together," Joseph answered. "You should be happy and rest well. There is much more to come. I am with you always. You are in the house of the Creator. We guard you as if you were the Temple of all Knowing."

Wow! I closed up my laptop and slept well. Without a doubt, this was the highlight of my week of writing in Three Rivers. With Joseph's assistance, the book was superbly launched. Too soon, it was time to leave. Driving out of town, I stopped for gas and an iced coffee with the coffee ice cubes that I had learned to adore over the last week. I fell in line behind a lovely woman, unknown to me, who asked, "Excuse me, are you Lee?" I thought I was in the twilight zone for a second as I only knew a few people in this area and she was not one of them.

"Yes, I am," I cheerfully responded. She explained that Christine from the art co-op had told her about me. She told me that her husband had a near-death experience, too. I asked if she was writing about that as she mentioned she was a writer.

"No," she said, but she soon came full circle to tell me: "My husband went to the gates of heaven and was greeted by these large, white whirling angels." As she was describing this scene, which I am sure her husband told her many times over, she paused and said: "We have a personal relationship with Christ, and it is exactly what we thought it would be. I am so happy that we are right." I encouraged her and smiled and agreed that it is an extraordinary gift to have experienced.

As I drove on, I thought about this interesting conversation. As we navigate this world we are constantly creating, we not only create what our reality is in this dimension, but maybe we create what we experience when we transition, too. This woman was so happy that her husband's near-death experience was exactly what they believed it would be and what they celebrate here on earth, and yet my experience, which was just as real and profound, was totally different. Were we both right?

CHAPTER 13 THE MYSTERY

Yesterday is gone. Tomorrow has not yet come. We have only today. Let us begin

~Mother Teresa~

We could hardly believe it, but Jean-Pierre had worked at the Westgate Taxicab Company so long, he was eligible for health insurance. We attended a meeting to discuss the benefits and sign up. It was the first time I had visited the main building, located in the heart of the industrial area just west of the Strip, and it was quite the awakening.

My body was having a physical reaction. The energy in the building made my skin crawl, and the inner vibration was making me want to scream and run out. As we walked toward the exit door, I got close to Jean-Pierre and said, "You have to get out! This place is consuming you. It is like the movie, The Blob, and, if you do not get out now, it will eat you alive." He laughed at my dramatic reaction, but he knew it was true. This job was consuming him. The darkness was winning.

Throughout my challenging spiritual adventure, Jean-Pierre has provided the most incredible support system I could ever imagine. But still, there is something that happens when two strong people marry. Sometimes you have difficulty "hearing" each other. It is an odd thing that I am able to converse beyond space and time but, more often than not, I struggle with my communication skills with my most cherished mate and husband. This was one of those times in our marriage.

It was late June, 2011 just after my trip to Three Rivers. "I brought you some ice water," I said, as I placed the glass on the spare bathroom counter while Jean-Pierre was in the shower. He used the spare bathroom that used to be my mother's room because he woke up so early for his taxi shift and didn't want to disturb me by dressing in our bedroom. I was thinking it would be nice for Jean-Pierre and me to have a few moments together, just the two of us. I wasn't expecting an argument.

"Are you mad at me?" I asked, after he did not acknowledge the ice water or a couple of conversational tidbits from me. It was 106 degrees. Just being in the house, the sweat drips off you. Due to our financial situation, the air conditioner was off limits except at night, when we put one of the two units in the house on 83 so we could fall asleep.

"Yes, I am," he replied. "Well, not mad at you; just mad about the situation."

"Okay," I said, as I went into our bedroom to take a shower and wash off the day as well. I didn't want to have an argument, not that anyone ever does, because I was tired and weary. I thought about what Jean-Pierre might say about me scheduling a landscaper to come and clean up a fallen tree and brush debris in our yard, and pull out weeds that, in some places, were knee high. I went over the details in my head as the cool water flowed over me. I thought about how it all played out and what I should have done differently.

Even with all my experience with self-healing and spiritual expansion, I still get caught in this web. As I moved into the kitchen after my shower, I heard: "Can we talk?" I hadn't even noticed Jean-Pierre sitting quietly on the sofa.

"Sure. Let me get this drink and I will come over."

Here it comes. We were going to have the classic marital dispute about money. Should our old landscaper do the yard work, or should we find someone cheaper? But the argument was really about the difference between what Jean-Pierre thought would be $100, and what turned out to be $400. Quite frankly, the job was worth far more, but our landscaper was cutting us a deal; that is how overgrown it had become.

Our house became an embarrassment to our neighbors and to me. I could not keep up with the maintenance on the house, and Jean-Pierre had lost all will to keep it up. It was depressing every time I walked in or out. It was feeling like we lived at the Munster's House.

In times of stress, Jean-Pierre and I cannot talk about money. He will tell you we NEVER have been able to talk about money. Not because Jean-Pierre can't talk to me about money, or I won't listen to him talking about money. The problem is, we have different beliefs surrounding money. My view is that money is energy, and it needs to be flowing to and from, keeping an image of ever-moving abundance. Jean-Pierre shuts down and worries about lack which, in my opinion, only brings more worry and more lack.

On this night, we moved on to petty nitpicking of each other's character traits until we reached a crescendo, followed by a long silence, some throat clearing, and uncomfortable body shifting on the couch.

"This widens the gap even further," Jean-Pierre said as his eyes started to deaden. "This is a central issue."

"Yes, it is," I replied.

"I must tell you that we are being deeply challenged right now," he said. Knowing that he meant our relationship was being challenged, I again said, "I agree." We were in deep here. But I have known that for some time; he was just coming to the realization. It was Jean-Pierre who finally came out with what we both had been leading to.

"I find that I do not like you very much these days," he said. I found myself not surprised by this comment. I had been feeling the exact same way about him. I affirmed the same sentiment back to him. We sat in silence. I was looking at Jean-Pierre, he was looking off into the distance.

"I need to go to bed," Jean-Pierre now said. "I have to get up early, and I have been up since 1 a.m.," as he walked toward the closed bedroom door without looking at me. I sat on the couch feeling the heat of the room more intensely now, with the sun dipping in the night sky reminding us to go to bed. I was waiting for the wave of emotion to rise up in me as it always does after a conversation like this. I replayed the pattern of the finale to past arguments.

Me sobbing. Jean-Pierre accusing me of emotional blackmail. Me warning him, "You should worry when I stop crying." That time was now. Tonight I had no tears.

The thought of dinner or sleep was out of the question. I texted our landscaper with an apology to cancel the scheduled work. It reminded me of all the times I had planned things that I had been forced to cancel. It felt like a power struggle. I then grabbed my laptop to spend some time with my thoughts, while Jean-Pierre and Luke slept. I pondered what had transpired this evening. After this intense argument, I wondered what it meant. Do you love him? What I knew for sure was yes, I do love Jean-Pierre. Is that enough? I am not sure. Is it enough that he loves me? Does he love me? Of course he does. Can love conquer the rest if the partners don't tend to their issues?

Answers eluded me. My thoughts kept circling back to the wonder and mystery of marriage and love when you stick out the challenging times with your partner. Yes, there needs to be gentleness, passion, compassion, kindness, and tolerance for sure. But I kept coming back to the love I felt for Jean-Pierre when I had my near-death experience. I was in awe of it.

Jean-Pierre talks about the storm that is above the sea. And, if you would just dive a few feet below the surface, there will be calm as it relates to relationships and quarrels. Just drop down below the surface a bit, and it will all be calm. There was something else at play here, though. Was the damage too much to recover?

I woke up early, knowing that Jean-Pierre had long left the house and was at least a couple of hours into his work day. He had been driving a taxi for months now, so that we would have an income while I worked long hours at the center building a place of healing for those in need. I made myself a cup of coffee. I like to call it "love in a cup," as it warms my inner physical form and nurtures my senses. Sort of like "love on a cone" but warmer and fewer calories. I said a prayer.

"Creator of all that is, I am accessing all the love of the Universe and acknowledging the immense power of the vibration. I gather this love energy and send it to my husband, Jean-Pierre, to heal any emotional wounds and release any denser energy that no longer serves either of us relating to our discord last night. Let him know how much I love him, and heal this situation with love."

I picked up my cell phone, dialed Jean-Pierre's number, and waited as the phone rang several times. It was 6:30 a.m. I was not sure if he would answer. But when Jean-Pierre's bright British accent cheerfully addressed me with a "Good Morning, Darling," I knew the Universe had heard me. "I will call you after I drop my passengers off, Jean-Pierre promised. Within five minutes, our conversation continued with Jean-Pierre thanking me for making the gesture to call.

I replied with, "Of course, I love you." The shift in the energy between us was tangible. We both chose love.

It is intriguing how this manuscript is unfolding while I am square in the middle of writing it. The final chapters of the book are being developed in real time, as if I am being guided along this linear timeline specifically for the results of the coming together of the storyline. It is fascinating to be within the story while writing it.

It was now July 2011. Jean-Pierre could not take one more day at the taxi job, and I thoroughly encouraged him to quit, as I always encouraged him to do what he loves and the rest will take care of itself. The job had lasted 10 months, and there was nothing positive about it except that it gave us an income, minimal, but still an income. It was time for a leap of faith on his part, and I was waiting for him to come to it himself. Jean-Pierre had been finding his voice over the last year in his graphic arts work and photography, and he was getting really, really good. It was his only escape from such a low frequency job. I was incredibly proud of him for sticking it out for as long as he had and for providing for the family, while we were working hard to build the center.

Jean-Pierre's photography is an art form in which he "paints" photos with his skill in digital color manipulation. He is so happy and passionate when he is doing it. His graphic arts work has developed exponentially, as he has designed book covers, invitations and collateral materials for the center and other clients. It was time for him to take his place at the center now, and I knew we would be happier being creative. One Sunday evening he simply said, "I can't do it anymore."

"Great. The Center needs you. It will be amazing."

By fall 2011, the pieces were falling into place for yet another expansion of Ganesha Center. We were preparing to move our growing operation from a group of individual rooms in an executive suite into an exciting new 6,000 square foot facility, tripling our size and expanding to eight treatment rooms, a huge meditation room, plus a café and small concert space. The grand opening was set for 2011's most auspicious date, November 11. All of this would fulfill guidance from long ago, before I opened my Reiki practice, when my Spirit guides pressed me to work toward a "big" facility by 2011. I have kept my pledge with hard work and the assistance of beautiful souls supporting the center.

Everyone at the center was working long days and buzzing with excitement. I was swamped with administrative duties and had stopped performing Reiki sessions and teaching. I missed it. There is an amazing feeling when I do Reiki or vibrational healing. The purity of connection and love, often for total strangers, is profound. It sounds odd to say love for a total stranger, but there is no other word. As I quiet myself and activate the energy to work through me, there is a connection of souls that is beautiful. I am in service for that person as the connector who allows them to remember who they truly are - an integral part of the whole. I am so grateful every session.

The look on the faces of our clients when they leave their Reiki sessions says it all. People are finding relief they have never known before in their lives. We hear from our members in floods of e-mails that vibrate with their thanks.

A member named Debra wrote: "I am so grateful that, in these times when spirituality is so badly needed on the planet, this wonderful center has been formed. If you are drawn toward spirituality or meditation, this is definitely one of the best places I have been on the planet."

Chanda wrote: "The incredible amalgamation of class and service offerings keeps me moving from one spiritual adventure to the next, constantly learning, constantly changing, evolving, and expanding. Thank you, Ganesha Center!"

Tom wrote: "If you haven't felt 'the light' before, or if it's been awhile since you felt love, you're sure to feel it here." This is what we would celebrate on 11/11/11.

As preparations for the opening continued, I took timeout for a quick trip to Baltimore to visit my mother and Delphine. Mom was living in the senior home facility Delphine had found for her, with friendly people, gorgeous grounds, and a private double room. It's true about time having a way of healing wounds. Enough time had passed. Mom and I were both looking forward to seeing each other, and we had a good visit. It was clear, though, that with Mom's deteriorating capabilities, this had been the right decision. Mom had settled in to her new home very well. She continued to complain, but that was Mom.

Back in Vegas after the trip, Jean-Pierre was kicking into high gear and assisting me with managing the household and Luke, as well as doing graphics and computer work at the center and for other clients. It may be short-term or long-term but, whatever it is, it will be perfect and predestined. The center was no longer an infant. It was a toddler that had learned to walk and now was getting ready to run!

In the days leading up to November 11, we all worked nonstop decorating, cleaning, picking up paint and paint brushes, making trips to Home Depot, installing baseboards, picking up paint and paint brushes, packing up the old space, managing inspections, and, did I mention, cleaning and picking up paint and paint brushes? The RSVPs were rolling in, and the buzz was starting about our new, larger location.

I was overwhelmed at times by the love and support of our volunteers. The level of anxiety and stress relating to the move was debilitating for me at times, and, if it were not for the incredible calm, hard work and support from our center supporters on those final days leading to the day of the opening, it would not have happened. When I say it was touch and go whether we would complete our new space in time for the grand opening that would be a huge understatement. By midafternoon on 11.10.11, there were 2,000 invitations sent, at least 100 RSVPs, our old space was packed up, we had furniture stored in a vacant suite, and no occupancy permit for the new space.

I sat in my car at a nearby park crying and cursing at the Universe. "I am sick and tired of this situation you put me through. I am working hard here, and all these amazing beings supporting this mission are so incredible, but I just can't take the stress any longer. I need a miracle here."

With surrender in my heart and the realization that on a holiday weekend, the ship already passed for the inspections to get accomplished by the afternoon, I pointed my car back to the old center to tell everyone we were going to have to cancel the opening party. However, the Universe wanted me to know I had been heard. In the late afternoon of November 10th, a miracle had occurred! The Great Day arrived, even more magical than we expected.

What a party it was! It was nonstop from 11:11 a.m. through 11:11 p.m., and there was never a lull in the crowd that which numbered in the hundreds. There was live music and entertainment at every hour on the 11-minute mark. The sense of community was never more present.

In the evening, we moved from kirtan and devotional music to old school R & B style inspirational compositions by songstress Edwige Binge. When she sang, "Reach out and touch somebody's hand, make this world a better place if you can," I watched as people instinctively moved around in a circle, at ease and inspired, in our new 2,000 square foot café and coffeehouse. Spontaneously, the guests started to hold hands, sway to the music, and sing.

I was so overcome with emotion as I looked around the room at all these people of every demographic. Young, old, gay, straight, diverse colors, races, styles, and beliefs, sharing the love and this day of celebration together as one.

Fittingly, the final guidance on my journey had come from Great Grandmother in a reading by Sharon Bridwell just a few weeks after the party. The channeling session turned into a few important threads of the story that still remained to be tied up.

I phoned Sharon on Friday, December 2nd, at 9:30 a.m. We exchanged pleasantries, and she welcomed in Great Grandmother and other Ascended Masters.

"Dear one, do not concern yourself with what will be arising," Great Grandmother began, somewhat ominously. Then, she offered only fragments: "Things will pass as quickly as they come in, within four days. A tear drop. Surrounded by a white cloud. Hearing the word 'change'. Don't worry. The fruits of the labor are soon."

All of this was puzzling, but what came next in two more fragments was clearer: "Seeing tall tree branches as if I were lying on the ground looking up. Now the book." It was especially interesting that Great Grandmother brought up the book, because I was going back to Three Rivers to finish writing it the very next week. Sharon did not know this.

More fragments from Great Grandmother: "Sit alone connecting with the earth just like you were a little girl again, lying on a blanket looking up at the sky. Even five minutes. Brings higher mind in connection. Creative thoughts will begin to flow. You come to understand about yourself and who you are and where you are going. How you are getting there and who you are taking."

Next, the subject changed from the book to the always emotionally-charged subject of our home. Great Grandmother had this to say: "I see a gold handrail along steps on a pretty good-sized house. I see a shield. Protection!" I was intrigued by the direction the message.

"Is this a house I will be living in?" I ask. "Yes."

Then Great Grandmother offered this prediction: "In

four days, (again with the four days, I thought) things are going to smooth out," she said. "Shifting is happening." As for the book, Great Grandmother couldn't have been more positive. "The book will be completed in this trip to Three Rivers," she said. "Let humanity hear the story. Your voice, the way you see it. Your higher mind. You can go and not worry. Go by yourself."

The hour had passed so quickly, as it always does, and I was left with a sense of awe once again. I thanked Great Grandmother and Sharon, sent my love, and concluded our conversation. I immediately went to find Brenda and Paul to detail for them the incredible channel that I had received. I carried in my heart a sense of peace and calm. With Great Grandmother's guidance, I knew everything would be fine.

We moved to my office so that I could speak from my notes on the session.   As I was finishing up, Jean-Pierre rushed into my office with a severe look on his face. I asked if everything was okay, and he delivered the news Grand Grandmother had now clearly foretold: "Our house sold at auction today, and we have three days to get out."

For most people, the announcement that your home of eight years was just sold in foreclosure, and that you must leave immediately just weeks before Christmas, would probably come as an enormous shock, maybe even an emotionally catastrophic one. But for me, at this time, I felt this house had done its job well.

It had protected us from the elements; gave our family warmth in the winter and coolness in the summer. It was the main location that provided a platform for immense joy and difficult lessons, and kept us housed and protected when we had no income. I loved in this house with more verve than I have ever loved. I cried in this house more profoundly and with a depth of pain that I had never known.

My beautiful child was conceived here with the union of love beyond space and time, as he chose his parents well. The Spirit world communicated with me here, and I awakened with a connection to God and beings that was previously just a possibility. I traversed dark, stormy mountains of personal and emotional obstacles, and came down the other side to find the ever-flowing sun shining on my face with peace and joy.

For me, the news felt like I had just won the lottery. Did I get the "numbers" after all? It was as if I just wrapped up a long-running play that was my life for this period of time. There was a sense of accomplishment and appreciation for the process. Relief that we had a good run, but it was time to move on to our next gig. I look back on the years in this house with all its hurdles and accomplishments with gratitude for the incredible journey. I not only survived it, but I owned it.

All the actors in my play who were main character parts, or had bit parts, were each so sweet in their delivery and involvement. Even the less likable roles felt beautifully orchestrated, as they gave me such growth and expansion. I see them all as significant to the entire theatrical experience of my life in that house. I honor all of them, as they honored me with their parts. The sentiment of closing this chapter of life was liberation and release.

When I tapped into my inner knowing, I sensed …. "Mission accomplished." When I asked, "What now?"

I heard … FREEDOM.

CHAPTER 14   CH-CH-CH-CH-CHANGES

With change comes transformation,

be open to the possibilities

~Lee Papa~

We were settling into our new center that was nearly 3 times the size of the old space, and not everything was in place yet. Yes, we had the grand opening party on 11.11.11 by a miraculous series of events … truly miraculous!

My deal with the Universe, and my unseen guides that assist me, was that if they pulled this off, I would shout from the mountaintops that a true miracle occurred. So, please help me visualize. Tall blond bundled up in the warmest clothes possible, a Sherpa earflap hat with dangling twisted yarn bits that look like braids hanging down in let's say orange and grey yarn.

There are white-capped mountains in the far distance. The sun was shining bright and reflecting off the patches of snow on the ground. It was bitter cold and just opening my mouth in preparation brings forth a puff of condensation. Do you see it? I take a deep breath, open my arms wide, lift my head, and shout from the mountain top…A Miracle Has Occurred!!!

Indeed, it had. The details of how this move came to fruition are so vast and filled with twists and turns that it would take another book to truly help you understand the depth of this extraordinary outcome; however, suffice it to say, we made it into our new space with the incredible support of the most amazing team of dedicated volunteers.

You know who you are and I am deeply grateful and the Universe blesses you 1,000 fold for your contribution.

We were still riding the high of the party, but there were significant logistics relating to the permits and finalizing the construction and fire inspections that needed to be accomplished. And we needed to fill this new place with seekers, students, and clients. I was overwhelmed! What an undertaking this all is. I found myself internally asking, "Why did you say 'yes' to all of this?"

After 8 years of collecting stuff, the idea of packing up a 2,500 square foot house in 3 days was daunting. Add to that, I needed to find a place to move to that was hopefully in the school district for Luke. His friends were in this neighborhood, and Christmas was only 3 weeks away. The look on Jean-Pierre's face as he gave me the update of the house being sold on the courthouse steps that morning was that of despair. He couldn't believe it, as the news had informed there would be a stay on foreclosures for the holidays. He was one big ball of stress.

"Jean-Pierre, give me the guy's number who bought the house. I will call him and take care of this. There is no way we can be packed up in 3 days, find a place to live and have a Christmas for Luke. Not going to happen. He will be reasonable." I could see some relief melting the grimace from Jean-Pierre's face knowing that I would handle it.

"What's his name?" I asked.

Jean-Pierre replied, "Zion."

"Are you kidding me?" I said. "Take a deep breath, let me work on this, and it will all be fine," I assured him. I was amused that the man I was to call regarding our house

… I mean his house … had a name that meant, "Heaven," in the Christian religion.

Just moments before the news from Jean-Pierre, Great Grandmother had given me the message that something big was going to occur, and in 4 days it was all going to be okay. If it were not for her guidance through Sharon, I would have been in a far more nerve-wracking space. I shared the communication that I had received with Jean-Pierre in hopes of soothing him, and when I took the details of everything off his plate, he began to settle.

It's what I do. I get things done. I overcome obstacles. Geez, I would really like to change that about myself and just let someone else do it. Or, at least not have any obstacles to overcome for a while. Smooth sailing ahead. Yeah, my new mantra.

Interesting, I thought, as all the messages that my guides had told me regarding the house were that everything would be fine, and the house would not sell in foreclosure until after we moved into the larger space. I had no idea it would be just a couple weeks after we moved, and that I would not have recovered from one move before I had to think about another.

Zion was tough but definitely had a gooey center. All in all, he was a kind man. I was grateful. After communicating our situation and the idea that all this was around the holiday, I requested that we could stay until the end of the year to give us a chance to properly move out, clean the house, have a Christmas for our son, etc. He finally agreed.

Next step … find a place to live. I quieted myself, asked for the guidance of my spiritual team, and asked them to direct me quickly to the place that would be optimal and easy for us to make the move. As usual, I referred to my go-to website Craig's List to see what the possibilities might be for a rental. I found a few options right down the street from our soon-to-be old house, and even closer to the park and Luke's school. I immediately made an appointment with the agent and asked Paul to make the trip with me to see the houses. It was bizarre and amazing!

Great Grandmother had said that the house would be full of light, would be a two story, and would bring abundance. Paul and I had driven to the house to meet the real estate agent at 1 p.m. We were sitting out front of the 2-story house with the rental sign that was directly across from the park - the address being 1313. As we were sitting in the car waiting, Paul joked about 1313 Mockingbird Lane as the Munster's address, but I retorted that 1313 was indeed quite lucky as if you add the numbers, you get an 8 ... the infinity symbol and a number for abundance. Ding, ding. Is that a marker? I later learned it also means the final point of manifestation and symbol of new life. The agent was not arriving, and it was 10 minutes past the hour, so I called him and he said, "I am here, waiting for you."

"No, I am here waiting for YOU." I laughed. "Where are you exactly?" I asked.

"1313 ... and he gave me another street name." I was confused. After a few minutes, we came to realize that he was on the street directly behind this street. What was going on, I wondered...this is strange. So, we headed over to look at the house he was representing. Immediately from the smell of the cigarette smoke in the house and the energy that was repelling, I knew this was not the house. We quickly left.

Paul and I got back in the car and drove to the house we had been sitting in front of just minutes before. There was something about this place. I began to get out of the car, Paul asked, "What are you doing?"

"I am going to see about this house."

"Of course you are," he laughed.

I peeked in every window I could find, but there was no clear access to peer in. There was no phone number on the sign, but I was not deterred. I went next door and knocked on their door. A beautiful, tall, dark woman answered the door with an inviting smile. I inquired about the house next door and she became even more animated and immediately called the landlord.

"The couple who own the house just finished with the renovations, and it is really beautiful. Are you interested in the house?" she asked.

Within minutes, Paul and I met the owner, and we were walking through this lovely home. It was so brightly lit up by the day's gift of sunshine. The paint, the carpet, and the tile were all muted natural tones and brand new. There was a backyard perfect for the dog we did not yet have, and it was spacious. Actually, too spacious, but it felt so amazing. The landlord was kind.

It was more square footage than we needed, but time was not on our side as we needed to make a decision pronto. I had come to honor my internal gut navigation and not second guess – as much – when all the signs are pointing a certain way. Having a house that energetically was incredible and was across from the park and near school were the 1-2-3 punch that confirmed this was the right place. Other than the size and price, it was perfect!

I called Jean-Pierre, who was down with a migraine, to come look at the house. He got himself together to tour it. As usual, in Jean-Pierre style, he was not overly enthusiastic, and I was hit with a stream of negatives about the house. I did not see the same. We did not have the luxury of looking around, and if I could make the financial terms works for the landlord and us, this would be our Christmas gift from God, Source, my guides, non-physicals, or whoever is out there watching over me/us.

This house was not going to be on the market long. The deal was done, another phenomenal situation beautifully orchestrated. Jean-Pierre expressed annoyance that the house was not right, but we had to move forward. I expressed irritation that if I didn't get this done, it wouldn't get done. And here we go again, I thought.

I so wished I had a partner who would be more positive and didn't see me or our lives as a push-pull. Sometimes, I just wished I had a partner that would take the lead. I was tired of being the strong one. I so desired a more positive, easygoing, and supportive union. If I heard the word "No" one more time before every comment or response to me, I was going to scream. In fact, I think I did on occasion - it was like a punctuation that started almost any dialogue. That word began to impact me so much that it was like an energetic shot that was fired when Jean-Pierre and I spoke. We were deteriorating; the gap ever widening.

The real hard work began. Jean-Pierre and I worked well together making the plan. We would move into the new house and set up as much as possible to make for a great Christmas for Luke. Then the next day, we would embark on a giant 3-day yard sale and be out of the old house by New Year's Eve.

We did it, but it took its toll. By New Year's Eve, we both went down hard. We got sick, really sick, and cancelled our plans for the evening with friends. We were ill for 2 weeks. I literally had no idea what was going on at the center, and I didn't care. I was wrecked. We both had strep and staph!

As I climbed out of the fog of physical exhaustion and illness, I found myself uncovering financial deterioration at the center. The process felt like what happens when you repot a plant in a larger planter. It takes time for the roots to fill in before the plant can grow. This was exactly what was going on at the center. However, we all rallied to increase funding through donations to the center and fundraisers.

We explored the non-profit status as an avenue, but after much research by many over a period of a year, we took the advice of a Masters Department Team from the Environmental & Public Affairs Department of UNLV and chose to stay with the same corporate structure. There were many opinions, as to how to run the center, and it was not always popular when the opinions were not followed. But what I did learn is that we all just do the best we can. You don't wake up in the morning and say, "I am going to do a half-assed job today."

Financial stresses continued. What was I to learn? Didn't I already go through this? The weight of the responsibility was heavy, and the weight of my relationship with Jean-Pierre was substantial. We were speaking less and less because I was tired of his lack of encouragement. It was like he wanted Ganesha Center to fail. During times of argument, he had said, "When are you going to stop this?" It only gave me more resolve that this was not about a job or a fleeting fancy; this was my life's mission. He did not understand it. How could he? I felt that there was some vein that went deep within him about his entrepreneurial efforts that did not come to fruition.

He was a shadow of who he was when I met him. He was traumatized; no self-esteem. No matter how I tried to lift him up with compliments about his incredible intellect and his talent, it didn't seem to help. Now I just felt like I was in survival mode, and I was alone at home. Jean-Pierre was taking the majority of the responsibility with house details and Luke, as he was not working a job, and I was struggling to make ends meet with the center and the house and was putting in a lot of hours.

The arguments were coming fast and furious in the new house, and it seemed that was the only time we communicated. When I would try to offer a story of the day, Jean-Pierre would interrupt me so many times that by the 3rd interruption I was weary to continue. This was not a new thing, as he did this more and more over the years, and it was hurtful. I grew tired of it and, even after expressing what I was feeling, he dismissed it as usual.

"You really don't know me, do you," he would say. "I can multitask. I heard you." To me, this showed no interest or respect for what I had to say.

Jean-Pierre was always "working" on something, but it appeared he was hiding in his office behind his computers in a world of creative expression that the world was not seeing. After he left the taxi job, we agreed he would pursue his passion.

"Jean-Pierre, your love is photography, and you are brilliant at it. You need to give this a real shot and make money doing what you love. Make a website where people can purchase your art, and go to networking events. Get business cards that you can give out, and I will display your art at the center gallery." I encouraged, encouraged, encouraged, and they were not empty compliments. I knew how amazing his photographs and art were, and I wanted him to be rewarded with financial success. But the art wasn't getting traction. It just appeared that his "working" was doing his art - not making an effort on the selling or marketing of the art.

By May 2012, Jean-Pierre and I were talking divorce and residing in separate bedrooms. On August 31, 2012, during the auspicious blue moon, I laid on my home office floor with arms open looking out at the night sky and offered to the Universe: "I am ready to move past blocks to my highest expansion." The next morning, Jean-Pierre and I had another argument. He had always been a gentle man, but he was internalizing so much anger that it was spilling out. I was done.

Neither of us was the best expression of ourselves in this union. We had come together for a wonderful purpose, and maybe that was complete. Our child was the greatest gift we shared. I did not want Luke to think that this was what a healthy marriage was to mimic in his life. Where was the nurturing, the consideration, the romance, the affection, the love? Long gone. What was left?

Jean-Pierre and I settled into the inevitable. We made decisions on how we would tell Luke that Jean-Pierre was going to move to the East Coast to live with his brother, and that we wanted to make this transition for Luke and for ourselves with love, respect and spiritually aware.

During this time, my mother was failing. I was receiving messages that she would be departing her physical state this year. Jean-Pierre and I agreed that, with my mother's impending transition, he would wait until November to leave for Connecticut.

Facebook Post October 2012:

Once again, I am sharing something very personal on Facebook. It seems that the old ways of doing things do not apply anymore in many facets of life, and this is one of them. In an effort to speed up the process of informing my friends, co-workers, acquaintances, Facebook friends whom I do not even know but feel connected to energetically through this field social media, and whoever else might read this post, my husband, Jean-Pierre and I are divorcing.

Divorce, Splitting-Up, Termination of Relationship, Dissolving of Marriage - these are words or phrases often used to describe the moving beyond the contract of marriage. They are also very charged with the imprint of whoever has had an experience, both positive and negative, with them when they are heard. From my experience talking with people, the charge is usually negative.

I would like to offer an alternative to these lower vibrational concepts: Karmic bond is complete; we are expanding into new growth horizons; allowing space for the fullest expressions of ourselves; Transformation; Growth, and so forth. Friends and family want to support you by saying things like, "I am sorry," "What happened?", "Is there a chance of reconciliation?" or even "You can't do this to your child!" These are all well-meaning, but not a match for today as we move so rapidly into higher spiritual awareness and love consciousness.

As far as our child goes, would it not be better to show him 2 households with loving, happy, fully-expressed parents as individuals than to be in a home with sadness, stagnation, and disconnection?

The beauty of 2 spiritually-aware people deciding that they no longer are the best expressions of themselves as individuals, and as a partnership in the confines of marriage, is the limitless possibilities of growth and expansion that wait. Honoring and loving each other enough to move beyond the limits of this label, working through the energy of pain, all the surrounding emotions, and coming through the other side with grace and love for all parties is our path and our intent.

Jean-Pierre and I came together 11 years ago, as was designed by the Universe, and we have gained immense wisdom and experienced so much love, especially surrounding our son, that there is nothing to be sorry for or regret. We are just moving into the next stage of our relationship.

I offer you this look into my personal life to make it easier for us to spread, but also to help others on this path of unions that no longer serve and are no longer a vibrational match. Instead of honoring this in a space of elevated thoughts and feelings such as love and seeing it as the gift of growth that it is, many fight it with negative words, hostilities, internal struggle, anger, resentment, disgust, etc., which only leads to festering within ones soul; "Taking poison and waiting for the other person to die," if you will. It only harms the initiator.

Please accept this as personal expressions of my life. I am in no way saying that my situation is the solution for everyone. I believe in the concept of marriage and know that there are rough patches to maneuver, and we certainly did that.

But there is also a time to review and to be honest with yourself to see if this life you are playing out serves everyone in it.

Just because our marital status changes on Facebook does not mean anything but that. The best bit is that we are friends! I thank Jean-Pierre for all the love, wisdom, and growth that came from every ounce of our daily being, and for being a wonderful father to our son. As we continue to create the life as individuals, always dancing in and out of the choreographed play of parenthood, we continue to support, love, and respect each other.

With much love and healing sent out to each one who reads this and the world.

Thank you!

CHAPTER 15   YOU WERE RIGHT!

The real voyage of discovery consists not in seeking new landscapes but in having new eyes

~Marcel Proust~

Seeing well-known medium and author, Hollister Rand, previously in action some months prior in front of an audience in San Francisco during a New Living Expo, provided me with the unwavering faith that she is indeed connecting to loved ones who have transitioned to whatever dimension or "other side" they reside once passing.

The idea that my mother had passed just the day before, and I would have an opportunity to be in the presence of a renowned medium, made me feel that there was something much greater at work here. I asked my deceased mother to pay me a visit if I was able to get myself together enough to go to the event.

You see, I was supposed to have been on an early flight to Baltimore, as per the initial plan. I had spent the afternoon, post the news of Mom's passing, crying in between the process of clearing my schedule enough to hop on a plane. The idea was that I would be with my family and assist my sister in finalizing arrangements for my mother's funeral and clearing out her apartment.

The Universe had other plans, or maybe my mother was rearranging the schedule. Who knows, but when my sister, Delphine advised me not to rush out and just sit with this a bit while we decide what the next steps would be, it made sense. Luke's 7th birthday was this weekend, and I so did not want to miss it.

This shift in arrangements allowed for some solitude and mourning time without being on task. I spent the day crying, and often uncontrolled sobbing, which surprised me, as my mother was 90 years old when she passed. We had been through hell and back together. I thought I had prepared myself for this change in her dynamics and the pain I had worked through regarding her living with me, and the move to Baltimore gave many opportunities for releasing sorrow and grieving. Here it was in all its glory - grief.

When Mom lived with us in Las Vegas for some years, we would have heart-to-hearts about her preparation for the next stage of her life…the afterlife. She was petrified. As devout as she was to her religion during her entire life, she was not prepared for her own passing. When we would talk about my visit in the Light during my near-death experience, I would explain that my newfound knowledge blew so many religious dogmas out of the water. There was nothing to fear. It will be a relief, parties, and a freedom like you have never known in this physical form.

Mom wanted to believe, but she had many, many years of programming to decode. We would keep it lighthearted, and I would say, "Well, that's okay because I know I am right. So, when you transition, I fully expect you to get your butt back here and tell me I am right. Do we have a deal?" I would add.

Mom would laugh and say, "We have a deal." There were variations of the conversation, but it always came down to me being right and us having a deal. It was a little private thing we had between us, and it was fun.

I had laid on the bed the afternoon of Mom's passing and asked her to come to me. I was not asleep, just resting and waiting. It was about 5 p.m. and the house was quiet. This is rare. Jean-Pierre had taken Luke to soccer practice, and everything seemed still. I had a vision of Mom as a younger woman, around 30-ish, floating over red poppies.

Mom, will you come to me? I want to see you," I telepathically told her in my vision.

"Yes, I will come visit you, but not now. For now you rest," she said. That evening and the next day were emotional release days. I figured with the vibration of mourning and sadness, there was no way my mother could lower her newly-found higher vibration enough to provide me with a visitation. However, as the day was progressing, I had decided that getting out of the house for our event with Hollister Rand would be a good idea. I wanted to appropriately greet Hollister, as this was her first event with us and we were sold out.

I didn't have to participate, really; just be there. I had not officially announced Mom's passing in any formal or public way, so only a handful of people knew about it at the center. I was not ready for the sympathy hugs that just might set me off all over again.

Hollister was on the small stage, shoes off, gushing with personality and engaging soulfully with 80 anticipating seekers in the audience eager to get a non-physical visit. I stood in the back of the room with our other staff peppered on the perimeter of the intimate room, and I was in awe of the connections she was making: touching her nose with her thumb and pointer finger as she was listening to communication from a world beyond our own, and pointing

171

and leading the individual to search their memory for clues that would connect the information she was receiving from loved ones standing behind, beside, or around the audience member. Signs and traces of information were being filtered through, building of a storyline or dialogue between the Spirit world and our physical world. Hollister was like the string between two paper cups.

We were almost to the halfway mark of the evening, and the break was eminent. I was finding great comfort in hearing loved ones pass on messages through Hollister of promise, love, and encouragement. The details of the individual's lives that were being revealed were incredible. Confirmation after confirmation of life after life filled the room, and the individuals there so sweetly drank it up.

I whispered "This is why we do what we do."

I use this phrase a lot when my Ganesha Center family shares an extraordinary story of release or newfound contentment, peace, or bliss from a newcomer to the center. It motivates us when we are weary.

Although I had some hope that Mom would visit, my need for it and anticipation was fading as the break became evident. We regrouped and settled in for another hour plus of this very entertaining communicator of other realms. We laughed; we cried; we were exhilarated. It was a magical evening, and I was glad I had come to be a part of this event. It was exactly what I needed.

I resigned myself to the fact that it was a lot to ask my mother, who just transitioned the day before, to make an appearance for me tonight.

"Maybe there is a sick bay that she needs to be resting or being decoded or something," I thought.

I decided to move from the back of the room near the restrooms toward the front left of the stage off to the side. My back was really starting to hurt me standing for such a long time, and I thought if I needed to, I could slide down to the floor and sit crisscross applesauce (those of you with children will understand what that means) for the others cross-legged. There was a moment of quiet as Hollister was connecting to someone. She touched her nose again almost pinching the sides as she moved her hand away and started to point toward the back of the room center aisle.

"There is an elegant woman walking down...." Her voice started to fade off, and I knew instantly with the words "elegant woman" that Mom had come. Hollister's voice came back to my conscious mind. As she was still pointing as if to indicate where the elegant woman was walking, Hollister moved her arm still pointing, and ends right at me. "And she is coming to you."

With a smile on her face, Hollister and I look at each other and acknowledge our mutual satisfaction that the connection was made. "She is a beautiful woman. Wearing royal blue. She said that blue was her favorite color." Breaking away from the translation, Hollister looks at me and says, "Lee, I know you said your mother recently passed."

I nod and stated, "Yesterday," and the room murmured. "But this woman does not feel like mother energy. She is saying that she never really felt like a mother." Hollister continues and says "She is saying don't make a fuss over her funeral."

I interject and say that it is already being done, and Delphine is getting it all together. The response comes,

"Well, she can do it, but do it for all of you - don't do it for me." Hollister begins her translation again,

"Your mother is saying that when she was here, she had a difficult time letting go of things. If she felt that someone wronged her in any way, it would be like a tape recorder that would play over and over in her head. She held grudges, she was tenacious. She says that this tape recorder is the first thing they took from her when she went to the other side."

"She is showing me her teeth and her jaw and is saying that she hated being old. Her cheeks were sunken in, and her teeth were bothering her. She hated getting old and didn't like old people. She would look at herself in the mirror and not recognize herself. She is saying that she was so tired. She could not take one more shower or bath. She is saying that there were mini-strokes involved with her decline, and that is what had been happening to her."

"Now she is showing me her hands and talking about rings." Hollister switched gears in the conversation. "What happened to her hands?" Hollister asked. I assumed that she was talking about her inability to wear her rings.

"Mom could not wear her rings anymore, as her knuckles were larger and she couldn't get them over them," I answered.

"She is concerned about her rings," Hollister adds.

Again, a validation of the personality of my mother. She liked her possessions and would be concerned about them in this life so, I suppose, although you pass into the higher realms, there are still personality traits that remain.

I add, "My sister needed to take my mother's jewelry home - she was concerned about theft."

"Wow, your mom was tenacious, and she is sucking the energy right out of this room," Hollister added.

"Your mother is hanging out here with a man. Is your father still alive?"

"No, he passed." I answered.

"She is with a man here who is still alive - your sister's husband?" she questioned

I add, "Maybe my husband?" Hollister confirms that Mom is acknowledging confirmation.

"She is there with your husband more than with you; she wants him to take a picture of her. Your mother is saying that you have a picture of her when she was younger. It was a beautiful photo and you used to have it up, but do not now."

The old guilt feelings of disappointing my mother came to the surface. "Yup, I thought...that is Mom."

"The photo was taken in a studio," she is saying.

"Yes." I shake my head in agreement.

"Your mother wants you to know that this is how she looks now. If your husband would take photos in the house, you will be able to see her there, the way that she looks now."

I add, "My husband is a photographer."

"Your mother is saying that she is with her mother and her sister on the other side. She is also writing a name for me." (A pause from Hollister as she is trying to make out the writing.) "L-O-I-S-E." "Louise?"

Hollister jokes that she missed a letter.

"Who is Louise?"

I explained, "Louise was a dear friend, I believe, when she was the age of the picture and they were girlfriends."

"I am hearing big band music." Hollister begins to sing the tune she is hearing. "Did your mother like to dance?" Hollister asks.

"She did as a younger woman probably with Louise, but my dad and she did not go dancing."

"I hear this music and she is dancing." she added.

Hollister is staying focused with me and my Mom for quite a while and I am so very grateful for the connection and communication. I was proud of myself that I was not crying during the exchange and just listening to what Mom wanted to share. Then she added, "Your mother is telling me that she was not going to disappoint you by not coming tonight." The tears started to well in my eyes as I pinched my lips together to hold back the potential deluge of emotion.

"And she wants you to know – you are right!"

CHAPTER 16   THE TEMPLE

Peace comes from within. Do not seek it without
~ The Buddha~

What I have come to know is that I know very little. However, I know what I know to be true for me. In my classes, I will tell my students that every class is different, as I am guided by the energies that are in the room. So, if they hear something that is not resonating, leave it to the side. It may not be for them, it may be for their neighbor. Take what resonates and leave the rest. In my opinion, spiritual expansion has nothing to do with intelligence or expertise. In some cases, intelligence is a hurdle that must be overcome to connect with Spirit or Awakening when it is used with a heavy hand.

I believe I may have an easier time connecting with Source because I am of average intelligence. I feel more than I think. I am not highly educated. I have not studied theology or religions of the world. I have the gift of a short memory, so I do not hold a grudge or hold onto old hurts. I have touched the Other Side, which allowed for the awakening that is my true self.

I am able to channel my inner knowing and non-physical guidance that assist me almost on a daily basis, as long as I allow it to be so. I am still learning. I continue to allow stresses into my life that kick me off course until I find my way back. I am in no way an alternative for your own guidance. I am a navigator and an advisor to access your own guidance - the guru within, so to speak.

My understanding is that the heart is where everything matters. Yes, the body and the mind are equally important, but use the heart to propel your lives. When you come to a decision, ask yourself "Am I in service?" "Is it nurturing?" Speak the truth from the heart and choose your words carefully as they have significant power. Your thoughts, words, and actions are in constant action to create your future.

In my journey, I learned that absolutely everything that "happens to me" is my own direct doing, and this is the same for everyone. We are not victims but creators of our direct reality based on the energy we are producing. It is the Law of Attraction. Every obstacle that I was surrounded by prior to my near-death experience, and after, are all ME. I am quite powerful to have produced such trauma and drama. Likewise, all the peace and joy that I have experienced is a direct result of my shifting with continued and constant inner work, spiritual development, and energy healing to move past limiting beliefs and energy blocks.

In my recent experience, I have learned that when you are tapping into your inner guidance, your Higher Self, your inner voice, and when you are traversing life in the frequency of love and light, you are in the "Slipstream." This is a beautiful, happy, joyful, peaceful place to maintain. Reviewing my experiences in this book was a cathartic gift. It allowed me to see the emergence of the peaks of consciousness in between periods of mind chatter, darkness, and attachment to this reality, and moments when I saw the light of spiritual expansion.

In this journey, I discovered the dark valleys of my past are a part of my growth, and so I could not condemn them. I had to accept them as what they are to my process, and continue to maneuver the experiences in life as rough gems to be polished on my road to higher consciousness, leaving judgment behind as an obstacle and a pattern of the past. In talking with friends and colleagues, I believe this is a blueprint for most spiritual seekers.

One of the greatest gifts you can give yourself is the time to be quiet and not just to contemplate on the past or the journey, but to allow the space, the silence, and the practice of being present that will reap great rewards.

Since 2008, my spiritual development has been mega-charged. When Luke was little, he would say Speed Racer Fast. I have lately become acutely aware of the global shift and the quest of self-realization amongst those who previously led their life with blinders, always moving rigorously toward the brass ring.

It is time for those who want to see and live in light to remember, and those being pulled in a spiritual direction, to heed the awakening process. It starts with baby steps – whispers, if you will - listening to your intuition, your guidance. It might be something like a feeling to read a particular book. While surfing the net, you are led to a particular website. Or, you open up a spiritual conversation with a friend and test the waters, watch for signs.

I love the stories from seekers who had come to Ganesha Center and how markers or synchronicity led them there. Some said coincidence or synchronicities, and others used messages to describe the process of awakening. We are all on our individual path to awareness and light energy. Release the judgment of self and others which can be quite the ongoing process and be patient with yourself.

Allowing this progression is quite rewarding. Honor another's journey or decisions, as they are necessary for them to get where they want to be.

These are historic times, indeed, and the movement of change will quicken as we are reaching the tipping point in our evolution. It does not have to be scary, and you do not have to live in fear of the unknown, or even what is known. Live in peace and love, and shine your inner light ever bright for others to see. Watch how things shift around you. Say "Yes!" more than you say "No." Affirm it! Swing your doors wide open for infinite possibility. If opening the front door to your spiritual house is too scary, just crack a window. You will find out very quickly that the love and light that is waiting for you, within you is you, and heaven on earth.

I have done deep soul searching over the years and have come to acknowledge all my experiences as Divine. Some are easier to acknowledge than others. Sometimes it takes me awhile to get to that place, but I eventually do, and I will continue to work on it with every new hurdle and experience.

They could be judged as good or bad experiences, or just as experiences to gain wisdom. To quote Oogway in Kung Fu Panda: "It's not good news or bad news...It's just news." Continuing in this vein, there are not good experiences nor bad experiences, just experiences; knowledge and wisdom to gain for continued expansion.

This is a tough ladder to climb and hang onto when life hands us up some major challenges. Even if you can only reach for just the next level of higher vibrational thought, you have gained something extraordinary. Celebrate it. The Law of Attraction is real. It was hard at work giving me exactly what I was creating - a difficult and challenging life between the years of 2003-2008. The more I focused on the difficulties and the self-doubt and destructive talk, the more it happily created that for me. Be your authentic self. Honor and cherish it. Speak your truth and love yourself. These are one of the best beginning steps I took in my awakening. Speak, act, and acknowledge truth; your truth, not someone else's regurgitated truth.

I leave you with this reminder from my Higher Guide Joseph:

"I am with you always. You are in the house of the Creator, and we guard you as if you were the Temple of all Knowing."

Soul-seekers, exalt in your awakening spirit and remembrance of your spiritual heritage. Exalt in your inseparability with God and with every other soul on Earth and throughout the universe
~Matthew via Suzy Ward, Illuminations for a New
Era~

In an effort to provide discretion for the players in my composition, I have changed the majority of the names to respect their privacy. As with every relationship and interaction, the beautiful force of perspective comes into play. How yummy it is to have so many different views on a subject, relationship, thought, life. But the most delicious of all, is to have perspective with no judgment.

My ex-husband and I found this too challenging IN our marriage but, beyond it, we work at it with love in our hearts to master allowing the individual perspectives as friends and co-parents of our beautiful child. With practice, everything becomes a habit.

I am grateful to Jean-Pierre beyond words, for with him, we created a canvas in which to mutually paint a parable of love, wisdom and spiritual expansion.

It was fascinating to explore the threads of parallels and synchronicities regarding limiting beliefs (I am not worthy, fear rules my life, I live in lack, etc.) and low vibrational traits that were woven through my life and this story. These little buggers are tough to extract out of one's existence. But, once you see them, and acknowledgement them, it is like an infection that must be removed or a computer program that needs a reinstall. However, what you resist persists.

Let me say it again ... What You Resist Persists! So, it is not about pushing these traits away. Start with the mirror and really look at your life. No victims here, only you. How might you be using these limiting beliefs or negative traits on yourself and in your daily life? Then, gently acknowledge and work on releasing and reprogramming them daily.

I use the technique of saying, "cancel - clear" after I catch myself in a negative or limited thought or expression, then restating the positive version of what I said or thought. As you make these changes, the old patterns will dissipate from your life. And those around you (family, friends, and co-workers) who may still hold on tight to these negative or limiting traits, may dissipate as well, as this is the Law of Attraction at work. It works in reverse, too.

You can attract what you desire in another vibrational level, as you release what no longer serves you.

I used the best of my ability to remember events as they occurred and, yet, I am certain with time and perspective, the recollection may be softened or more rugged, depending on my mood or my viewpoint on the events. This manuscript has no malice intended; I hold nothing but love for every single performer in my lifelong theatrical play. I am grateful for each experience, as it helped me grow enormously, and I am who I am today because of all of them.

The purpose of this book is to inspire, provide hope and crack a spiritual window or a door to the idea of just how powerful we are as creators in our own lives.

The experiences in this book are not for the gifted or for the few. These and many more are accessible to ALL. It is your right. Slow down, explore and uncover the awakened you. You will simply be astonished.

The more I stay focused on the present, the more challenging it is to recall the past. This is part of the blueprint of the exceptional life of all knowing, as the temple is you, and all of us.

The magnificence of a practiced open heart, living in gratitude, living in the moment, exercising forgiveness and staying focused on love is that in your own personal journey to bring knowledge, wisdom, and love back to Source – We are One.

One of the many lessons I learned with spiritually navigating my life is that there is nothing more constant than change and that is something to be embraced, not resisted. This is where growth occurs. The first channeled information I ever received was "With Change Comes Transformation, Be Open to the Possibilities."

And I fully allow this to unfold as my life's mission has expanded to globally inspire and assist those awakening to Mind – Body – Spirit transformation.

Since the creation of the center, over 4,000 individual classes have been taught and thousands of individual private sessions were realized within 5 years. Ganesha Center was a visionary for Mind – Body – Spirit wellness in Las Vegas. The ripple effect of assisting tens of thousands of individuals on their path to optimal spiritual health and physical well-being brought Ganesha Center to transform its recognized expertise to the corporate and consulting arena.

We accomplished this by converting the focus from a stand-alone wellness center, to assisting corporations and individuals in establishing that space for themselves within their organizations and cities. Our extensive knowledge, partnership development and referral base, makes us the ideal company to guide you personally and professionally to your wellness goals.

You can contact Lee Papa to schedule your Transformational Advisory Session, a Book Signing, Lecture or for your Key Note speaking needs at lee@leepapa.com or lee@ganeshacenter.com.

11812046R00106

Made in the USA
San Bernardino, CA
30 May 2014